CW01210552

ELENA

A Life in Soho

ELENA

A Life in Soho

ELENA SALVONI
WITH SANDY FAWKES

Q

Quartet Books
London   New York

First published by Quartet Books Limited 1990
A member of the Namara Group
27/29 Goodge Street, London W1P 1FD

Copyright © by Elena Salvoni and Sandy Fawkes 1990

The moral rights of the author have been asserted

British Library Cataloguing in Publication Data

Salvoni, Elena, *1920-*
Elena, a life in Soho.
I. Title   II. Fawkes, Sandy
647.95092

ISBN 0-7043-2745-7

Typeset by Input Typesetting Ltd, London
Printed and bound in Great Britain by
BPCC Hazell Books
Aylesbury, Bucks, England
Member of BPCC Ltd

*To my dear husband Aldo,
who has been my strength*

One

Most of the people who are lucky enough to discover Soho fall in love with the place. For them the love affair often starts in early adulthood, when the world seems like a giant sweetshop or playground. For me it started a lot earlier and has been more of a marriage than a love affair, with all the responsibilities for better or for worse, and, like my real marriage, it has lasted a lifetime. A lifetime of hard work, true, but a happy one.

Mama was a first-generation Italian who didn't speak very good English, so all our childhood troubles would be taken first to Dr Rampagna in Gower Street, then on to Mr Fortuna, the Italian chemist in Frith Street. The Italian–Soho connection was already well established and Mama would gossip with Mr Fortuna while his niece made up the prescriptions or would order camomile flowers for her tisanes or belladonna plasters for her back; women worked very hard in those days, doing the washing in great coppers, mangling, ironing, doing everything by hand. And I would just stand there gazing at the great pear-shaped bottles in the window filled with green, purple and reddish liquids.

Mama, who still wore long skirts and lacy blouses and always had a shawl over her head, would then take me round to Gennarro's, a very grand Italian restaurant in Dean Street which is now the Groucho Club, to visit friends who worked in the cloakroom and the linen department. On the way, there would be people in the street to chat to, people from our district, Clerkenwell, all of them making a living in Soho. Then it would be back by bus, a number 38 or 19, along exactly the same bus route that I use to get in and out of work some sixty-odd years later.

Soho has seen a lot of changes over those years. Mr Fortuna's is now the E & G Stores, an Italian provisions shop, where I can still keep in touch with news of friends. The Bar Italia in Frith Street is very popular with the young and there are boutiques and shoe shops where there used to be butchers, wine shops and grocers. These days there is more money about, but the spirit of people striving, creating and enjoying themselves is still alive at L'Escargot in Greek Street and I hope my presence has helped maintain that spirit.

Yes, there are differences and the most difficult one I had to adjust to was writing people's orders in English when L'Escargot opened in June 1981. For thirty years I had worked at Bianchi's in Frith Street and before that at the Café Bleu in Old Compton Street, places where the chefs were Italian and understood my writing. I was sixty-one years old and had to learn to adapt; just as dear old Soho herself has always done. Though I no longer wait at tables the job of welcoming customers and taking their orders still gives me immense pleasure. My routine is very simple. I catch the bus from Islington at a quarter past eleven every morning and when I arrive I go straight to the upstairs office to talk over the events of the night before – like who was in and whom they were with (sometimes the kind of information I wouldn't dream of passing on elsewhere, and won't be revealing in this book either, so it is quite safe for my customers to read on!) Then it is downstairs to Elena's

Room where I check the state of the tables and, my favourite bit, the bookings. Each day is bound to be different, but to see that an old friend has booked a table is a treat; I have made so many friendships during my years in Soho and some of them run into three generations so I know I am going to catch up with family and career news, a lovely feeling.

L'Escargot has three floors of restaurants, the downstairs is a brasserie, fashionable and not too expensive for young careerists, my room is on the middle floor and above is a glass-domed room with a portrait of me and another of Aldo, my husband, by Kay Galway. My 'pitch', as it were, is between the two top floors so I can greet everyone and direct them to their tables, checking that they are happy where they are seated, very important if people want to discuss business.

All round the room are framed photographs of the people I've watched over with love and affection; they are famous now but it wasn't always the case, and I am as proud of their success as if they were my own children. I brought many of their pictures from Bianchi's as they were personal gifts to me: a treasured one of Tony Hancock who always sat at table 15; Beryl Reid who was also first taken to Soho by her mother; Elaine Page who was interviewed in Bianchi's before the opening of *Evita*, so nervous and shy it was worrying to see. Happily all went well and she gave her last-night party for *Chess* at L'Escargot, surrounded by her family and friends as well as the cast. She's a hard worker that girl and I've often had to send food round to the theatre because she can't get out to eat; but that was never a problem; as someone who started work at the age of fourteen I've always admired a grafter.

On opposite walls I have pictures of Vincent Price

and Coral Browne. I asked them for a photograph, meaning one of them together, but Vincent Price sent a photo of just himself from Los Angeles. When Coral Browne discovered this she deliberately sent me one of herself alone, too. I hung them separately and it is a joke they both enjoy. There is a picture of Cleo Laine and Johnny Dankworth, whom I always called Frankie in the early days as he was so thin and looked just like Frank Sinatra, and a lovely one of John Hurt whose fortunes were at a low ebb for such a long time. I realised then just how difficult actors' lives could be and this is why it gives me special pleasure to read about them doing well. There are photographs of many more – all of them reminders not only of the happy times that Soho has given us but also, as in the case of Nick Tomalin who was killed in the Yom Kippur War in 1973, of the fact that friendship often has to bear the burden of sadness.

Among the pictures is a charming reminder of my first day at L'Escargot. I was terribly nervous; well, it was a lot posher than anywhere I had worked before, with specially designed carpets of navy blue with snail trails all over and borders of fat little green and yellow snails. As for the pale-green walls, Francis Bacon was heard to complain that they made the place look like an ice-cream parlour. (He has since overcome his objection as the food is so good, but I know what he meant.) It was all unfamiliar and very impressive.

We opened on 2 June 1981, and although every table had been booked by old customers from Bianchi's I was still a bit scared. There is a curious feeling as lunchtime begins: people have been working all morning, they are tense, sometimes they are meeting complete strangers and it is only when I hear that unmistakable sound of people enjoying themselves that I can relax. Luckily that day the customers were as pleased to see me as I was to see them and I had already got them settled when David de Keyser, a dear actor friend, came up the stairs with a single red rose. He couldn't stay, but it was such a sweet gesture that I felt immediately at home in my new premises in Soho. Also there were Sandy Lieberson and Alayne Stewart, the heads of Twentieth Century Fox. Now, as I say, it was our first day and apparently the skip with the rubbish was still outside. In it they found a tiny off-cut of the carpet's border which they lifted and returned four days later in a frame, signed on the back. It sits between Nick Tomalin and a picture of Prince Andrew's Rolls Royce which has a snail as its mascot.

I met Prince Andrew through Norman Parkinson, and I met him through an old customer of mine from Bianchi's, Tom Hawkyard, who told me he was repaying a forty-year-old debt. When Tom was assistant art editor at *Vogue*, Parks introduced Tom to Soho by taking him to Leon's in Wardour Street. 'He used to call me the undertaker's nark,' says Tom cheerfully, 'because I was very skinny and bought my suits from Burtons, which was all I could afford on my *Vogue* salary.' Well, Tom is no longer skinny and his job as consultant to 3M brought him back in contact with Parks when he had his first major exhibition at the National Portrait Gallery.

It was Norman Parkinson who suggested to Prince Andrew that he hold his Kodak exhibition at L'Escargot, and it was when I was seeing him to the door that I noticed his snail emblem outside on the car. Since then he has been back to dine with friends on several occasions; there is no fuss, but I do have to keep a table by the door for his bodyguard. It is the same when any of the Royals come for an evening. When Prince Edward comes in with friends after the theatre, there is always a letter of thanks accompanying the bill. When she was very heavily pregnant, the Duchess of York came in for lunch with Prince Edward and her friend Biddy Heyward who works for Andrew Lloyd Webber, as does Prince Edward. At the top of the stairs she was out of puff and turned to me and said, 'It's all right for you, you're used to it.'

Which of course I am, and proved it by being sponsored for a week going about my duties. It was for the Wishing Well Appeal for Great Ormond Street Hospital which needed money to provide accommodation for mothers with children in hospital. It is a cause dear to my heart. One of my earliest memories is of my two older brothers being ill in bed. As it was the custom then to place a bowl of fruit beside them, I nipped upstairs and pinched a bunch of grapes. These I was sharing with my friends in the street when the doctor arrived. When he had finished examining the boys he called me in and took a swab from my throat. Soon after that an ambulance drove up to the house, a great event in the street, but instead of taking my brothers they bundled me in. I had diphtheria which was a dangerous disease in those days and I was taken to the Fever Hospital in Hampstead; it was very frightening being surrounded by lots of nurses in starched aprons and lace caps, but the most scaring part was when Mama came to visit me wearing white overalls and a mask.

Years later both my daughter Adriana and my son Louie had to go into Hospital to have their tonsils out and I'll never forget the distress I felt at having to leave them. It has taken the medical profession a long time to learn that children need their mothers when they are ill and so I was determined to help Great Ormond Street. I attached a pedometer to a garter and told my customers; I even boldly gave them a glimpse, probably the first time any of them had seen my knees. I raised £8,500 in that week. I had walked fifty-three miles. £7,500 went to the Appeal and the remaining £1,000 went towards the purchase of a house in Gray's Inn Road to be turned into flatlets for mothers with other children, in recognition of the fact that an illness in the family affects everyone.

My customers' response had been instant as I knew it would; they are a warm-hearted lot and most of them have known difficult times themselves. I was reminded of that the other day when Maeve Binchy was launching her latest book at L'Escargot. The first time I met her was when she came to Bianchi's to meet someone from television. I suggested that he would want her to have a drink while she waited and so she accepted one. I could see she was anxious and thought it was probably about the business they were going to discuss, so I brought her another drink as he still hadn't turned up. Finally she went to the phone and discovered there had been a mistake over the date, his or hers I can't remember, but she was worried about the drinks; I said I would put them on the bill next time. Weeks later she told me what I had already guessed, that she had been sitting there without a bean on her; it's good for a laugh now that she is such a success.

We have lots of parties and launches at L'Escargot, either in the high-ceilinged Banqueting Room at the front or upstairs in the glass-domed Barrel Room, and the very first private party we held took me right back to the early days of Bianchi's when I got to know the mother and father of the bride whose party it was. Her parents are Judge Nina Lowry and Judge Edward Gardner, and Aldo and I were invited to their daughter's wedding which was held in the crypt of the House of Commons with a reception afterwards on the terrace. There we met up with lots of their relatives and friends, like George Baker and his wife Sally; it was all very glamorous and great fun. In the evening the bride and groom, Sally and Adrian, threw a party for their young friends in the Banqueting Room of L'Escargot. Being accepted as part of their extended family made me feel good and reminded me of my own youth when all Mama's friends were aunties and all their children my cousins. It couldn't have been a better start to another decade of fun and festivities.

Somehow even the business parties keep up the old connections and one, given by Shell for executives from all over the world, helped establish the Italian–Soho relationship in our new place in a most satisfactory and happy manner. An old friend, Barry Dugdale, was the host; he had once given me a mirror printed with the double-headed figure and the Shell slogan, *'That's Shell, that was.'* It hung in Bianchi's and so intrigued Rod McKuen, the singer, that he offered me any amount of money for it. I refused to sell, and the proof that money can't buy the love you have been given lies in the fact that the mirror still hangs in my hallway at home. Brian Dugdale also gave me a little gold shell on a chain a few days before L'Escargot opened, so when he asked for live music, including a piano, for his party I set out to do all I could to oblige him. Reluctantly, I had to tell him in the end it was impossible. Getting a piano up and down the stairs and at the same time organising the three other restaurants for lunch and dinner and then getting it out the following day just wasn't practical. I suggested an accordionist instead. I grew up with the Binelli brothers and knew how good they were; Michael plays for all our church reunions and Ettore has been a sessions man, often doing background music for jingles. Cautiously Brian agreed to give it a try and Ettore played very softly during dinner a great range of tunes. One by one the guests asked him if he knew such and such a tune, in many cases their national songs. Ettore was able to oblige them all and the evening ended with everyone doing the Highland Fling and singing *Auld Lang Syne*. Now Ettore plays at all the Shell parties.

I needn't have worried about L'Escargot being too posh; my dear old hooligan friends may have gone up in the world financially but their behaviour and ability to enjoy themselves in the early eighties was pretty unimpaired. There was a crazy evening when Des Good organised a stag night party for Brian Griffiths. They were all in the television commercials business and Des, as best man, wanted to make it something special. He decided that the party, held in the Barrel Room, should be on a theme of Officers and Tarts. The men (boys I should probably say) hired turn-of-the-century uniforms and marched in formation up the stairs through all the restaurants. Everyone thought it was a regimental dinner, including Lee Remick who was dining in my room. She was fascinated and asked which regiment they belonged to. I didn't like to disillusion her and say it was only a party so I promised to find out. Half an hour later the Tarts arrived, all girls from the advertising agencies dressed in feather boas and sequins; they were supposed to be delivered at the door in a coach, but it couldn't get into Greek Street so it had dumped them in Soho Square. The sight of them marching *en masse* up the road had caused much astonishment to passers-by; maybe they thought it was a counter-demonstration to the Festival of Light which was staged yearly at that time by feminists protesting about the exploitation of women in Soho. Later, Des had to go out to locate the coach and when he got back I told him Lee Remick wanted to know about the regiment. 'For Christ's sake don't say a word, Elena. I've just been out on the street wearing this ceremonial sword and I suddenly realised I could be arrested for impersonating a member of Her Majesty's Forces.' So I never could oblige Miss Remick with the information, but everyone had a good time and I found out later that Des got Brian to the church on time – just.

Another great joke happened on Shaw Taylor's sixtieth birthday. He was having dinner with some friends when two big plain-clothes men came in and said they had received reports about a gentleman here impersonating Shaw Taylor of *Police Five*, and that was against the law. Before I could protest they had handcuffed him and carted him off to a waiting police car. There was much consternation in the restaurant; nobody could imagine what he had done and there was already a crowd outside on the pavement – as there always is whenever a police car stops in Soho; I daresay there are quite a few who are thankful it isn't their turn to be bundled into it. I rushed down the stairs to see if I could be of any help only to see the flashing lights haring up the street. I hurried back up the stairs and found his guests laughing themselves silly. It was a put-up job. He had been kidnapped and taken to a surprise party at Scotland Yard. What a relief.

What a relief too when Gaye Brown and her Rock Bottom group won their case against Thames TV. Of course my loyalties were torn in two as many of the Thames executives are my friends. Jack Andrews has the same birthday as me, and he and Liz Isherwood sent me two dozen white roses and came to lunch on our opening day. Nevertheless Gaye, Diane Langton, Anabel Leventon and Don Fraser had done all their planning at Bianchi's and their recording in Soho. They told me they had met up at an audition along with Wayne Sleep, another of my regulars, and had gone off for a drink together and out of the conversation the idea for the group grew. They were a marvellous crowd. They always had a large table filled with friends and musicians, all good-humoured, never a row; not very well off but full of vitality. It took them ten years to win their case and at the end of it they threw a party at L'Escargot for all the friends who had supported them. They took over the ground floor and sang all their original songs. Joanna Lumley was there and David Shilling, who had designed an outrageous hat for Gaye with an enormous ostrich feather which walloped everyone in the face whenever she moved as she is six foot tall. They all told me what they had done with the money: Gaye had bought a house in Wandsworth, Anabel had bought one in Primrose Hill, Don had bought Elgar's studio in Bedham in Sussex and Diane had bought herself a pale-blue Rolls Royce. Oh, it was fun to see them so happy and as I stood outside waving Diane off in her Rolls I felt really proud of them all. They had guts.

Although I work the two upstairs floors I usually get a message if there are friends eating in the brasserie and pop down to see them. One evening, after the first night of *Iolanthe* at the Phoenix, Gaye had a large table of friends over by the window. Among them were Barbara

Steele, who usually plays the beautiful vampire in American horror films, Peter Straker, Danny Fisher and Ned Sherrin. Gaye was, as usual, laughing and she told me that Ned, having found the front door shut, had tapped on the window which they had opened to let him climb in. As he did so, with a certain amount of help, he was followed by four young black chaps dressed in leather. Now, all the company thought they must be some musicians Ned was working with and made them welcome, but Ned had never seen them before in his life. The poor bewildered chaps looked round at this hooting and very gala company and promptly clambered out of the window back into the street.

I sometimes think of L'Escargot as the bigger house I needed for all my children to keep coming back to with all their friends. Lots of them come back to celebrate achievements that were hatched in Bianchi's. Ed Victor took the whole of the ground floor for the fifth anniversary of having set up his own literary agency, a decision he had made while sitting at table 5 at Bianchi's. It was a packed and jolly affair as he is very popular; Janet Street-Porter was there with her then husband Frank Czitanovich, Deborah and David Owen, Paula Yates and Bob Geldof, Gaia Servardo, Michael White, Tony Delano, Andrew Logan and Nigel Dempster; what was so lovely about it was that they were all old customers of mine and friends of each other – it made for a great atmosphere. Even the fact that Stanley Reynolds gate-crashed the party (a throwback, after all, to everyone's sixties' habits) didn't upset anyone; he was in fine form and made immediately welcome. The following day I had a sweet letter from Ed saying how thrilled he had been and that from then on he was going to tell everybody to hold their parties at L'Escargot. I think he must have been as good as his word as we still organise several a week.

It must be said that my children are a good-mannered lot. I receive so many letters from them when I've arranged an occasion. Robert Kee after his seventieth-birthday party wrote a note of thanks because we had all stayed late, and he enclosed a gift to the staff which was a very charming gesture. Michael Fenn sent me a letter of apology because he had forgotten that he owed me money for a meal he had had in Bianchi's; he'd gone to America for a few years but on his return his friends had reminded him; he sent me a cheque for the outstanding amount plus interest, which was a nice thing to do and the fact that the cheque was ten years late made it even more endearing.

What people don't realise is that if they welsh on a bill it has to come out of my pocket; another thing they don't realise is that I have a fantastic memory for faces. This came as quite a shock to one man recently when he arrived early at L'Escargot. I greeted him by name and could see immediately that he didn't know whether to be flattered or embarrassed to be remembered. I was just about to tell him the reason when his hosts arrived; perhaps I should still have told him that he owed me money; it might have saved his hosts a few bob because I found out later he was notorious for swindling people in a very businesslike manner. Fortunately such people are rare in my world. At least I can be sure he won't be back.

My friends and customers like to share their triumphs. For instance, there was the time Arnold Saltzman rang from downstairs in the lobby and asked me to come and look at his Oscar. Well, I popped down thinking he wanted to show me his dog as they aren't allowed in the restaurant, but he was alone and I looked at him all puzzled. He pulled a bag out from under the table, opened it for me to peep in and said, 'Look, Elena, I've won an Oscar.' And there it was, all gold and gleaming; he was taking it to be inscribed. He told me that David Puttnam had won one too and they had clinked them together on stage because David had started out as Arnold's props boy. I was thrilled for them both and very touched that he should have thought of me, and I ran round the restaurant looking for someone with a camera and we had a picture of the three of us, Arnold, Oscar and myself, taken on the steps of L'Escargot. I was especially happy that Arnold had kept in touch with David and Sandy Lieberson when they went to Hollywood and was able to tell me how they were getting on. Fortunately both Sandy and David had taken my advice when they were offered their high-powered jobs and had not sold their houses over here. There had been no back-biting when things went wrong, and my attitude had been that they should bring the money back into this country and get on with helping the film industry here.

Another nice thing about my friends and customers is the way they look after their families, a very important quality to me. Michael Palin brought his mother in for her eightieth birthday then afterwards flew her to America on Concorde as a treat. He and Eric Idle both have a great sense of humour; they tease me mercilessly and can twist anything I say into something funny.

It is also lovely when the people I have known for many years bring their grown-up children in. I've usually seen pictures of them over the years and we have plenty in common despite our age differences. One evening Judi Dench and Michael Williams gave a party for their daughter Finty's sixteenth birthday and invited a group of her friends. They were all having a lot of fun when Hal Prince came in and, hearing all the laughter, asked what was going on. When I told him he asked me to take a bottle of champagne over but not to say where it came from. I did so and Michael said, 'But we didn't order champagne, Elena.' I told him that if he and Judi looked across the room they would see where it came from. Of course they were all old friends and there was much kissing and hugging and everyone had a wonderful evening, but Judi told me later that the kids didn't make school the next day. It didn't surprise me.

There was a reunion of a different kind at one of the book launches we hold quite frequently; it was between a young girl of long ago and Larry Adler. The young girl was me. Aldo, my friends and I used to line up outside the Holborn Empire before the war to see him and I told him so when he came to a party. He was enchanted to be remembered from the days he trod the boards, and when he heard that Aldo, too, played the harmonica he dived into his pocket and fished out a miniature mouth-organ inscribed with his name and presented it to us. It is in a little presentation box and still sits on my sideboard, but I have to keep it out of the way of my grandchildren because it is so small they could swallow it.

Another reunion was very sweet: an old customer from Bianchi's told me rather nervously that he was meeting his daughter for the first time in sixteen years; at the time of his divorce from her mother arrangements were not as civilised as they mostly are now. When an event of this importance takes place one has to be very, very tactful. Such a situation calls for a mixture of making people feel comfortable and leaving them alone to get to know each other again. Sometimes a third person can help just by being chatty, so I told her I had known her father for many years, found out that she was a nurse and said that now she had found her way here she would always be welcome. I know that nurses don't earn a lot of money but I haven't lost my skill in conducting people through the menu so they don't spend more than they can afford.

I will admit that I do get sentimental about some of my customers; I truly love being their confidante and being part of their lives, and what surprises me is that they think I will have forgotten them. How could I when they have shared some of the most precious parts of their lives with me? Like Dr Parker who came to L'Escargot one evening with a lady friend having told her about the good times he had spent at Bianchi's. I hadn't seem him for four years but the moment he came up the stairs I remembered the evening he had passed his exams. I had known him since he was a somewhat impoverished medical student, and that evening he whispered to me that he had just become a fully fledged surgeon and he was about to tell his mother whom he had invited to dinner. She cried with joy, a moment of love and pride and affection I felt privileged to share. Now he is the head surgeon at St Stephen's in Fulham Road.

I have been the first to know about many engagements and sadly, over the last two decades, about many divorces too; although a break-up of a marriage distresses me I've learned to cope with the bravado people have to put up. There has to be a sense of loss even if it doesn't always show. Patti Boyd came in after her divorce from Eric Clapton, with her friends Ringo Starr and his wife Barbara Bach, and behaved impeccably; if she shed any tears, which surely people must do at the end of a marriage, she didn't do it at the table. But I expect she was grateful to have such good mates; it can't be a great day to go through alone.

The strangest feeling for someone with a poverty-stricken background like mine is to be sorry for somebody who is truly, seriously rich. It happened one day when an absolutely beautiful young couple came in and asked for a corner table; I knew the man and his brother too, they both spoke exquisite Italian. The man said, 'Do you mind if we don't eat? We just want to have a drink together.' I told him it wasn't possible, the restaurant was running to capacity. He replied that they would pay for a meal but didn't want to be disturbed. That was OK by me; I could see something was brewing between him and his lovely companion, so I served them wine and left them alone. About half an hour later his brother came in accompanied by a rather short dark-haired woman whom I vaguely recognised. All I heard was 'Oh, my God' from the man at the table as he cringed into his drink. I knew something was wrong but there was nothing I could do about it; soon afterwards they all went off having paid for two lunches and the wine. It was only as she went down the stairs that recognition clicked; it was Christina Onassis, and the man who had arranged the clandestine meeting with his stunning girlfriend was not Italian at all, but the Greek heir to a shipping fortune, Nicky Mavroleon, with whom Christina was desperately in love. He was equally desperate to escape her clutches. Poor Christina Onassis, it was the first time I ever understood the cliché, 'Poor little rich girl'.

Someone who thoroughly deserved to be a poor little

rich girl but wasn't was Caroline Kennedy. One evening she came to Bianchi's with a whole bunch of students and Derek Shrub from Sotheby's. They had a marvellous evening with nobody disturbing them and Derek told me later that she had written to her mother to say what a smashing restaurant it was; I doubt if we will ever see Jackie herself in L'Escargot, but it was nice to have been host to President Kennedy's daughter.

Now, most of the Americans I meet are very well behaved. Usually over here to talk business, they are cool and charming, but David Carradine was an amazing exception. Over the years I've learned how to calm people down, usually by insisting that they eat before talking any more, but there wasn't a lot I could do when Carradine and his then wife, Linda McGuinn, got a row really under way. Apparently they were barred from every smart restaurant in Hollywood and after their performance in L'Escargot that night I could understand why. They were outrageous and I was horrified; they looked as if they would come to blows. At that time David Carradine was a wondrously cool Kung Fu character in a television series, a kind of oriental Robin Hood, who sorted out the baddies from the goodies and won battles for the under-privileged through a mixture of peace and strength. Well there certainly wasn't much evidence of peace that evening. It looked as if he was going to hit her and I was concerned that my customers might be upset enough to go to her rescue – Michael Ivens was already half way out of his seat. So I marched up to them and told them to pack it in. What, I asked him, had become of the famous patience that we watched every week? It worked; they apologised and quietened down but I'd been very worried Michael Ivens was going to find himself on the receiving end of a Kung-Fu chop. I read recently that David Carradine has changed his wife and his drug-taking habits, but the article also mentioned that he is being sued for having injured somebody in a restaurant with a karate-style attack – so my instinct wasn't far wrong.

I'm still settling business arguments, too. I can see them brewing out of the corner of my eye. The simplest way to nip them in the bud is to rush into the servery, get their food up quick and, in best motherly fashion, tell them to eat it all up. The method relies upon a Pavlov's dog reaction, memories of their own mothers; but they obediently set to and by the time they get to the coffee-and-brandy stage it's all blown over.

Happily there is more laughter than disaster. I thought it was very funny one day when Melvyn Bragg came hurtling out of the gents saying he'd just had the fright of his life. 'I was standing there, Elena, when this man came in, looked at me and said, "I'm from the Police." I've never zipped myself up so fast, though why I should have felt guilty I don't know. Then this man said, "Don't you remember me, you interviewed us on television."' It was Sting, the lead singer with the Police. Dear Melvyn, he's taken a lot of flack from the gossip columnists because he is good-looking, successful and talented, and if it gets him down he doesn't let it show, but I still think it's amusing that he should have exactly the same reaction as the rest of us at the mention of the word 'Police'.

I thought Nanette Newman was funny, too, when she went hurtling into the servery mistaking it for the loo. I went chasing after her and perhaps I should have said 'No, No, Nanette' but all I could think of was her ads for Fairy Liquid! I was concerned because Brian works the servery like a piston engine and if he'd barged into her there could have been a ruined dress and a ruined meal. As I dragged her out I said, 'Haven't you done enough washing-up for one day? I thought you might like a rest.'

Now I know it might be considered a bit unkind to laugh at people when they get a bit intoxicated, especially if you're not a drinker yourself, but there are times when it is either laugh or wring their necks. And the night a gentleman was convinced that his wife had been abducted in Greek Street was one of those. The man and his wife were guests of an old regular from Bianchi's. They'd all had a very pleasant evening when the wife asked me to call a cab as they had to catch the last train home from Waterloo. Farewells were said and husband and wife went down the stairs together. Quite what happened next I was never altogether sure. I assume she got into the car while he was sorting out his coat. Anyhow, the next I knew he came roaring up the stairs screaming that his wife had disappeared and that she was probably being cut into little pieces right at that moment. There was no calming him down. I think he must have grown up on a diet of B films or comics and still thought the white-slave traffic was operating from this den of iniquity called Soho. I tried saying she had probably gone ahead because she was worried about the children or the dogs, but his only reply to any kind of sensible suggestion was to shout that he was a member of the Stock Exchange and a very respected man in his field. He then insisted I call the police, something I was reluctant to do – not for our reputation, you understand, but because he stood a good chance of ending up in the cells himself. He wouldn't be the first respectable member of the Stock Exchange to do so. Finally I rang the police and two coppers came round and caught the situation at a glance. There was poor Mr Stewart, his host, trying to pacify him with the offer of a glass of whisky which was refused ('I can't drink while this terrible thing is happening to my wife') and all the time he was taking great swigs out of his friend's glass. Eventually Mr Stewart persuaded him that they would be better off waiting for any news at his club, the Cavalry, and the police, trying to keep straight faces, promised to do all they could. They had attempted to explain that nobody could be put on the missing list until they had not been heard of for forty-eight hours but, as I have learned over the years, you cannot reason with a drunk, however 'Hooray'. Although I was sure nothing untoward could have happened to his wife, I made them promise they would ring me as soon as they had news and, sure enough, at 1.30 a.m. there was a call saying she was safe at home; she had waited at the barrier till the last minute, then caught the train. It was hysterical and when those of the remaining customers who had watched the whole high drama in disbelief heard the news, we all collapsed with laughter.

Thank Heavens there weren't such goings on the day Sir John Gielgud came in for lunch with the director of a film he was making. They hadn't booked, and the only table I had was right in the centre of the room; this I offered diffidently as I thought he might not like being stared at. I know I can rely on my customers to be pretty blasé, but Sir John is rather exceptional. In the end it was he who was surveying the room. As he left he said to me, 'I must congratulate you. You have brought this place alive and it is wonderful to sit in a room with both the young and the old enjoying themselves.' In their own inimitable way Peter Cook and Dudley Moore echoed Sir John's sentiments when they came in for dinner during a rehearsal for the most recent *Secret Policemen's Ball*, a show they organise for charity. Their version was, 'Everywhere in Soho is so naff nowadays, thank goodness L'Escargot is still a nice place to come to.'

I'm glad they think so, though I don't know too much about the other places except what my customers tell me, and I'm far too busy to go gallivanting myself. I still go home to see Aldo every afternoon for a chat and a cup of tea. For years Aldo worked in outside catering for Fortnum and Mason, but the hours were so punishing, going on until two or three in the morning and then starting again at eight, that eventually his health broke down and he had to spend some months in hospital. When he recovered he took charge of the cash desk at Bianchi's; then he came with me to L'Escargot to the cash desk here. He often listened to the customers' problems well into the night – so he knows all the people I am talking about. He retired when the management brought in computerised bills. Now he stays at home when I leave to get the bus back to work around a quarter past seven in the evening. It's lonely for him but he rings every night around midnight to see if it looks like being a late night and I pass on the messages from customers who have asked about him. They all love him.

I no longer catch the late bus home; it's not that I think it too dangerous – when you've grown up in Clerkenwell you can deal with the streets – but I am getting on a bit. At one time the management paid for my car home; then along came the tax man saying it counted as a company perk and promptly charged me £3,000 in back tax. So now I pay for my own cars (I'd rather see my money go into some hard-working driver's pocket). Aldo always waits up for me however late I am and we have another chat and another cup of tea just while I unwind. As soon as my head hits the pillow, that's it. It's a full and happy life.

Two

A few months back I walked down Eyre Street Hill, a little curved road not far from St Peter's Italian Church on Clerkenwell Road; it was a sentimental journey and I counted the gratings in the pavement until I came to the place where, on 29 April 1920, I was born, and where I lived for the first seven years of my life. Then I crossed the street, went up the hill a little and gazed in turn at the house where Aldo was born and lived for the first seven or eight of his.

The area is derelict now but the memories are as vivid as ever; it was a wonderful street filled with life, noise, the smells of cooking and the vitality of a close community. The houses were small, jam-packed together with front doors slap on the street and always open. I suppose we were all poor but as children we weren't aware of it and we were always welcome in each other's houses.

Mama and Papa were both orphans from Northern Italy and had been sent to the Italian community in Clerkenwell when quite young – which must have been a daunting adventure in retrospect. They were gladly taken into people's homes and by the time I came along there were aunts, uncles and cousins galore. I had two older brothers and one younger, but my sister Juliet died the year before I was born. Poor Mama; she kept a lock of Juliet's hair wrapped in a black-edged handkerchief which I still have, but when she grieved she never let me see it. The neighbours would tell me what a beautiful child Juliet had been. It was many years before I could appreciate that Mama must have been more frightened than I was when I was rushed into hospital with diphtheria at the same age as Juliet. The hospital sent her a telegram to ring them urgently but it was delivered to the wrong house; then, when it found her, poor Mama, who spoke very little English, couldn't understand what it said and, of course, had no knowledge of how to telephone. The only telephone in the whole area belonged to a grocer (who was also a bookie) and it was a very brave neighbour who went to his house and asked to use the phone to take the message that I was past the crisis. Mama was eternally grateful to her but apparently many women from the street were shocked that she should have entered that man's house. It all seems so strange now when people carry phones and use them in the restaurant! It was many, many years before we even had one at home.

When I came out of hospital I discovered that Aldo had been there with diphtheria, too. Being children neither of us knew how long we had been in but it must have been weeks because Aldo's hair was shoulder-length when he came home. What our parents must have gone through!

And how they worked! Papa was an asphalter working on roofs all over London and Mama ran a boarding house so the lodgers became aunts and uncles too. Aldo's father sold ice from a horse and cart. He bought the ice from a factory underneath the arches at Waterloo and Aldo remembers riding with him sometimes and being proud that the horse knew every stop. I have a very vivid memory of us having to be quiet in the evenings as Papa had to go to bed early in order to be up at four to walk to work in the East End during the General Strike of 1926. Fifty-three years later during the transport strike I found myself doing the same thing. Papa would have been proud of me.

I suppose I learned to work hard from Mama's example; there were no such things as mod cons in those days. The toilet was out in the back yard and the washing was done in a huge concrete copper in the scullery. The water had to be poured in from buckets and a fire lit under it; when the sheets had boiled they had to be lugged outside to be mangled, then hung on the line to dry, then folded and ironed with a flat-iron heated on the kitchen range – you had to spit on it to see if it was hot enough. The kitchen stove had to be cleaned with black lead and polished till it shone like a mirror; rugs were hung on the line and beaten by hand and the lace curtains, bought from Indian door-to-door salesmen, had to be bleached and starched.

No wonder those women had backache. On top of everything else they had huge meals to prepare. Food was invariably home-made and the pasta, the sauces, all had to be ready to serve up when the bread-winner came home. Mama made wonderful risottos and my 'auntie' across the road made gorgeous pizzas so we would eat in each other's houses: it was a marvellous childhood. The area where we lived is a small triangle between Clerkenwell Road, Roseberry Avenue and Farringdon Road, and we children knew every inch of it. Wandering round I can still remember who lived where just as when I look at our old school photos I can recall the names of all the children.

St Peter's Italian School was on Herbal Hill. The building is still there but it is now St Catherine's School of Dance. To think it once housed twelve hundred of us – a mixture of Italian, Greek, Irish and English. We all learnt English at school. I suppose we must have picked up some in the street because I remember the skipping-rope rhymes like 'Silk, Satin, Cotton, Rags' (whichever one you tripped up on was what you were going to be married in). The streets were completely safe – nobody would have dreamt of molesting a child – and because they were entirely free of traffic we could stretch the heavy brewers' ropes right across the road for our games. We played five-stones (jacks), hopscotch, overbacks (leapfrog) and hide-and-seek all round the streets.

It was the tradition in all working-class families for the girls to help their mothers round the house after school while the boys were free to play as soon as they got out. The boys were all football mad and, since there was no money to spare for anything but the essentials of living, they made their own footballs out of bundles of newspapers tied up with string. These must have been as effective as the real thing because Joe Bacuzzi went on to play for Fulham and for England in the first international match against the Russian Dynamos after the war; a picture of him being presented to King George VI still hangs in the Coach and Horses, Back Hill, just down the road from St Peter's Italian Church.

Sunday was the great day of the week and still is; people come from all over London to attend Mass. Italian Catholics are a devout but cheerful lot and St Peter's is a splendid church with huge marble pillars and filled with paintings. Based architecturally on an ancient basilica in Rome, it was built in the latter half of the last century and I was christened, confirmed and married there. It has always been, and still is, famous for its music; Benjamino Gigli often sang with the choir before the Second World War and other performers from La Scala, Milan, the Opera of Rome and the Opera of San Carlo in Naples have sung there since. The school was right next to the church and every Thursday afternoon we would go there and be exhorted to sing as loudly and lustily as we could; it must have done me good because I have taught all five of my grandchildren to sing *Papaveri* along with Gigli and they love it.

The church was the centre of our lives but not in a dominating, miserable way. I still go to a service every Sunday but more often now to St John's at the top of our road in Islington. There are still old schoolfriends who keep St Peter's polished and dusted and arrange the flowers out of love and respect. Every week people who have been to Mass end up in the Coach and Horses afterwards, for a drink and an exchange of family news. Although there has been a pub on that site since the sixteenth century it was always known to us round the area as Resteghini's after the man who owned it from 1921–77 and was the first man in London to get a licence to sell wine because that was what his Italian customers drank. In medieval times it was a tavern famous for bear-baiting and cock-fighting, and they say Dick Turpin's bag was found in the cellar and that Charles Dickens based his character Fagin in *Oliver Twist* on a real-life customer who used to send the local kids out thieving. I learned all this from Brian Phillips who now owns it and has the old Italian connections even though he comes from South London originally. The few remaining residents are always welcome to play *briscola*, a very noisy card game, and reminisce about old times.

In my childhood all the local families crowded into

the church every Sunday morning for Mass and afterwards would stand in the street greeting each other. We were all dressed in our Sunday best, the girls and Mamas in hats, of course, and the boys and Papas in suits and ties. As children we were expected to be well behaved and if we attempted to interrupt a grown-up conversation we were told we could talk 'when chicken does wee-wees'. I've never quite understood that remark but whatever it meant it worked, and we kept our little traps shut.

Presently, the women would head for home to prepare Sunday lunch while the men drifted off to the clubs and pubs, all close to each other, where they played cards or bowls. There was a bowling alley at the back of the Gunmakers Arms a bit further down our street which Papa particularly liked. When the meal was ready we would be sent out to fetch them: there was never any problem as in those melodramatic Victorian tales of children standing desolate outside pubs begging their fathers to come home. We had wine with our meals – watered because we were little – and sat round a great big table with Mama's lodgers. After lunch (though it was called dinner then) the street people selling cockles and whelks from barrows would push their way round the streets calling their wares. Then there would be the muffin or crumpet man with a big wooden tray on his shoulder, the bagel man, who used all his profits to play dice, and the catsmeat man. Every family kept cats, mainly for the practical purpose of keeping down the mice which otherwise would have flourished in such an overcrowded area, but they were loved and cherished and fed on horse-flesh – not out of tins like now.

It was a great neighbourhood and nobody would have starved while there was still enough flour in the larder to make pasta. It was also a time of great innocence for children; the day I was led upstairs to meet my new baby brother I was quite unprepared and his sudden appearance was a complete surprise to me; nobody would have dreamt of mentioning how such things came about in front of children. Funny when you think that kids nowadays are supposed to accept homosexuality in both sexes as soon as they can read. I was seven at the time and hadn't noticed a thing; and afterwards I don't think it ever occurred to me to ask where he had come from. A few houses down the road another baby was born about two weeks later but the baby's father was killed in a tram accident and the child's mother lost her milk; Mama, who was a placid woman and had plenty, fed them both. How marvellous those women were! They looked after each other as well as everyone else. As children we were never made to feel in any way a hindrance; we were the blessings of life.

If my parents quarrelled, and I daresay they did – nobody can manage a lifetime without falling out occasionally – I never knew of it; the only violence I can remember in my life came from one of our teachers, Miss McDermott, who used to wallop us round the head with a hefty book if we weren't paying attention. It makes me laugh now with all the arguments about corporal punishment in schools; I can't imagine what an education minister today would make of the school's decision to transfer her from the boys' department to the girls' because she was so fierce she frightened the lads – and they weren't milksops either. (They used to dare each other to jump from the iron bridge in Farringdon Street on to Back Lane below. Our parents would have had fits if they had known.) But the other teachers were gentle nuns; there was Sister Margaret, the headmistress, in her big white hat like a butterfly, and dear Miss Kelly who died only a year or so ago aged ninety. We all went to visit her at the hospice because all of us, her pupils, had stayed in touch with her all our lives.

We meet up every year at the Italian procession for the Feast of Our Lady of Mount Carmel which is held on the nearest Sunday to 16 July. In the past the streets were garlanded, people were packed as many as twelve deep on either side of the road and the girls wore long white dresses and veils. There were so many of us in the neighbourhood, the procession could be a mile long. It is a simpler affair these days but still a great gathering point for the old community. There will be Louis who runs Annabel's in Berkeley Square, Georgie T (Boy T as we called him – we all had nicknames) the grandfather of Tony Hadley the lead singer in Spandau Ballet (and still called Boy), and so many more of us, all exchanging news of families, friends and work.

We've all done well but we aren't ashamed of our humble background, far from it. We love to reminisce about things like the tramrides we used to take to Hampstead Heath for picnics. We would catch the tram in the Gray's Inn Road, go up past Kings Cross and end up at South End Green, just opposite the Playhouse. It was all perfectly safe, we didn't need adults to supervise us, and at the end of the day every scrap of paper would be packed into the basket and taken home; nobody dreamt of leaving litter – if we ate even a sweet in the street the wrapper would go into a pocket until we got home. I'm not sure about the crumbs from the halfpenny bags of broken wafers we bought from Charlie Petti's factory, but I daresay the birds took care of them.

On Bank Holidays we would go to the Hampstead Fair, again on our own, something parents wouldn't risk allowing today, with sixpence each to spend – and, oh, the pleasure of agonising over what to spend it on. Considering the level of poverty at the time, our parents were very generous – although we didn't get pocket money, just treats on special occasions. And for me those special occasions were visits from my godfather on his Sundays off. He was the *maître d'* of a West End hotel and Mama had nursed him and three other lodgers during the great Spanish Flu epidemic of 1919. He used to give me 2/6d when he saw me, but if Mama saw him first she would tell me to buzz off, she wasn't having me cadging.

In the summers we would go to Felixstowe for our holidays, again just the children of the street; Dr Rampagna ran a holiday home in a great big house by the sea and for one guinea a week, which our parents must have had to save up, we had fresh air, sunshine and swimming. We wore black woollen bathing suits that never seemed to get quite dry but as we ran in and out of the sea we didn't care. There would be Aldo and his sister Anselma, Mary my best friend who was born in the same house as me as her mother had married one of Mama's lodgers, and many others . . . probably about thirty of us altogether. Dr Rampagna's house was beautiful and the grounds seemed enormous to a child from the backstreets of London. In the late twenties there was a strong movement towards health and fitness so every morning we were out in the grounds doing physical exercises, all in unison, jumping up and down and waving our arms about. At the end of each session we had to march past the doctor and his wife with our right arms raised and fists clenched; we did as we were told and had no idea that this was the Fascist salute which was to have such sinister significance later in our lives.

During the rest of the year the school used a sportsground in Edgware; for weeks one particular year we were drilled for a parade before Mussolini's daughter. Aldo was in the band playing *umpa, umpa* on his tuba but all I remember is that she wore a cowl-neckline dress, a large picture hat and had a great big hooked nose. So much for politics.

Somewhere around that time the *Daily Mirror*, which was on Farringdon Road then, used to run competitions for teams of health and fitness dancers and photograph them on the flat roof of the building – which shows how acceptable the general idea was at first even if later it was to be interpreted as subversive.

Most of the time we were just getting on with the business of living, passing our exams and enjoying ourselves, and so were our parents. Any birthday or anniversary was a cause for celebration and our streets rang with the sound of the accordion and singing, rather than political haranguing. Christmases were wonderful. Mama would make a great feast of ravioli, rolling out the pasta on the scrubbed white-wood table in the kitchen; I'd help cut out the little squares with the coggedwheel tool and there would have to be four to five hundred of them as the lodgers would all be joining us. People did not pop back to Italy for Christmas then; the reason they came to London was to find work, send some money home and save so that when they returned they could start up their own business. Nobody expected to take two weeks off from work, so Christmas Day was a real holiday; except for Mama whose work was never done and who would turn the leftover pasta into spaghetti and dry it over the washing line. Sometimes we would have capon, but never turkey, and we didn't have a Christmas tree until my daughter was a few years old.

Our presents would be something that we needed, like a new coat or dress that we would parade in at church in the morning, and something to eat – always an orange and some nuts; also we were not expected to give anything in return. There certainly wasn't any money for toys but none of us felt deprived; nobody else had any so there was no competition. I did once have a celluloid doll from Woolworths and there was an occasion when I won a gorgeous china doll at a street party (having had to fight some big bully of a girl for my ticket); she had golden curls (the doll) and chubby knees. Mostly we made our own entertainment with guessing games and so on; there was a form of spoof where you put your hands under the table with fingers folded that Italian men played – you had to be terribly quick and I think it taught you honesty. It certainly taught you laughter.

The reason why people worked so hard was that they wanted to move up in the world. I suppose it's still the same. Our own achievements were modest; when I was nine we moved up the street from number 21 to number 8 which had been the landlord's house. He and his family were moving up in the world. We didn't need a Pickfords' van, just the help of the neighbours. Our new status symbols were an inside toilet and a copper gas-fired boiler in the yard – which meant we could heat the water for the tin bath without sweltering in the summer. We still had no electricity round Clerkenwell. A nightmare for any child was to be sent to the shop to buy a gasmantle; I would say the responsibility was about as great as delivering £50,000 in cash nowadays. They were very fragile things made of a sort of woven powder suspended in a cardboard box and they cost 1/6d each. If the slightest damage happened to them on the way home you were to blame. You didn't even speak to a friend, you just watched the pavement and the box because the tiniest break in the network meant they wouldn't function. It was an ordeal that was only over when the thing was installed, the match lit, the tap turned on and there was light.

Mama's boarders moved with us to number 8 and by 1933 she and Papa had saved enough to buy a house in Islington, the house where I still live, about a mile up the road from Clerkenwell. I still went to St Peter's Italian School and to evening classes as well, oddly enough in order to learn proper Italian as our parents spoke with a broad dialect. We used the evening classes as a social occasion, learning to mix with the boys as the sexes were separated both in classes and playgrounds during the day. We were growing up and most of us would be going out to work within a year but there was no such thing as biology lessons, let alone sex education. I don't think we even talked about it amongst ourselves but I suppose we girls must have learned about periods from each other. Certainly none of the teachers would have mentioned such a subject, nor our mothers either, but then young people have always eventually found out these things for themselves, otherwise there wouldn't be a human race.

I imagine that in every group of schoolkids there is one girl – and probably a boy too – ahead of the others. My shock came from my friend Julie. We used to do an odd job cleaning a house in Vincent Terrace to earn pocket money on Friday afternoons after school. We would take the washing to the bagwash and dust and polish the furniture and the brass fittings round the fender. We were both terrified of the huge dining-room which was dominated by a vast oil-painting of a Roman soldier; we always made sure we were never alone in that room. We earned 2/6d each for our efforts, which was really quite generous, and the lady of the house also gave us scrambled eggs and tomatoes for tea. She was very elegant and we would watch her sail off to dinner in her finery and black satin shoes; how I admired them. Even so it took me right up till last year to buy myself a pair but very proud of them I am.

It was some time after I had started work that I popped round to see Julie on a Saturday; there was pandemonium in the house. Her Neapolitan grandmother was wailing at the top of her voice, her mother was shrieking, and I thought something dreadful had happened, which, in a way, it had. Julie had given birth to a baby. I went up to see her and there she was with it in her arms. I didn't know what to say as I still didn't know where they came from, and somehow it didn't seem the time to ask, but I did find out that the chief source of grief was the fact that the father was a young English boy. Funny to think of it now when very grand and well-known people are proud to talk about their love-children. It may have been that event that prompted my father to say to me, 'If you ever have a problem, come to us, don't go to anybody else, nobody here is going to shut the door.' And Mama's philosophy was always that if you can't do anyone a good turn don't do them a bad one.

Three

In the summer of 1934, at the age of fourteen, I left school and a week later I started my first job. Now, in a close community like ours nobody ever had to go to the Labour Exchange to find work; the fathers would look round among their friends for an employer for their sons and the mothers for one for their daughters. We all went into trades, none of us into domestic service. Mama wanted me to be a seamstress. I had learned to sew in my last few years at school and the daughter of one of Mama's lodgers worked in the West End for a Mr Arnaldi of Dorville Models in Mortimer Street. I was petrified that first Monday; Mr Arnaldi's workrooms made elegant, tailored suits and dresses and my sewing experience was limited to things like pin-tucking, hem-stitching and double-hemming. I sat next to Olga and watched her every move. My first job was marking up with long loops of thread and then cutting out very carefully; we all wore white arm-cuffs so as not to mark the material. All of the eighteen employees had different skills. Like all beginners I was the tea-girl too.

I earned 7/6d a week and gave Mama 5/- of it. It was expected of all young people then that as soon as they went to work they should help support the family. Now it seems the other way round and the kids expect to spend all their money on themselves. I went to work on the number 73 bus and the fare was 2d. I walked home to save the pennies to buy fully-fashioned silk stockings for the weekends – a great extravagance at 1/11d and, oh boy, did we look after them! A run was a disaster.

Of course we took sandwiches to work and I'd bolt them down to I could go and browse round Bourne and Hollingsworth's in Oxford Street. Oxford Street was very grand then, lined with large department stores with assistants who called you 'Modom' and sold everything from beautiful pure-silk underwear trimmed with hand-made lace to ranges of sewing-thread in every shade imaginable. How I enjoyed those lunch-hours. I don't remember ever feeling the smallest pang of envy for those who could afford to swan in and buy whatever they wanted.

We had an hour off for lunch and punctuality was very rigid. You didn't get paid when you were sick, either. We had a half-day on Saturday, finishing at noon, and then it would be off to meet up with my old school-friends to compare notes about our new lives. The others were all apprentices in something like hairdressing or catering and Aldo, because of his love of sport, was making shuttle-cocks. On Sundays after Mass my girlfriends and I would go window-shopping, sighing at the tall, beautiful mannequins and imagining ourselves in the clothes; funny really because most of us were small and going to remain so. But as I advanced in the workrooms I became able to copy the clothes in the shop windows. Mr Arnaldi would let us use his patterns and we'd go to John Lewis for our materials and work through our lunchtimes, all helping each other. Everything had to be saved up for, shoes, handbags and accessories very carefully chosen and equally carefully looked after, clothes brushed and pressed and shoes regularly polished; well, when you have saved up 12/6d for a pair they had to last.

I had worked my way up to 22/6d a week when I joined up with a former employee of Mr Arnaldi's, Nimfa Di Maggio, a distant cousin of the famous baseball player Joe Di Maggio, who had set up her own business designing and making wedding dresses. I seem to recall that our first job together was making the wedding dress for Miss Tollemarche, the daughter of a rich brewing family who was marrying Sir Thomas Beecham's son. I also seem to remember it was my first encounter with how difficult and awkward some people can be, but it certainly wasn't my last. I'm afraid we were an empty-headed young lot then, only concerned with what we were going to wear to the weekend dance.

Even though several of our families had moved up to Islington we still all met at Ted's Cafe in Clerkenwell. We gossiped and chatted but we never talked politics; we had too much news among ourselves to bother about the great wide world outside. Perhaps it was also because our community was too multi-racial to be prejudiced. We had Catholic Italians, Jewish Italians, Greeks, Irish and English. When you grow up in such a close-packed society you learn to respect other people's habits be they religious, eating or dressing. We simply couldn't comprehend hate and so ignored it. We couldn't very well call each other names, could we? The Scots called us names though. They'd shout 'spaghetti' after us or sometimes 'Wops' or they'd yell, 'Italians sell fish, three halfpence a dish', at us; at the time we couldn't understand why and it was much later that we found out that almost every Italian who went to Scotland opened up a fish-and-chip shop.

Still, name-calling didn't worry us kids and to prove

it there were later on many marriages between our different races. At that time though we just all went dancing together, sometimes at our old school hall which cost a shilling and sometimes at the Finsbury Town Hall which was half a crown. The girls wore long dresses and silver shoes, which they always carried in a bag to the ballroom – they were far too precious to risk getting them scuffed on the street. We all sort of taught each other to dance, though I learnt a lot from my cousin Louisa who had been crazy about Rudolf Valentino. She would parade about in a large black hat with a red rose behind her ear, very much the Spanish senorita, and grab me as her partner for the tango. I was only about six then and I suppose I thought she was half-mad, showing off on an ego-trip; it was only later when I remembered all the steps I realised how lucky I had been.

Aldo wouldn't come to the dances at first, he thought they were cissy and he was much more interested in sport. He'd been part of the school football team and they had lots of trophies. For cricket he had won a Jack Hobbs bat in 1933, a great achievement (we still have the framed certificate). But he was still part of our gang and we persuaded him to come along one day. We were all young, around seventeen, so we didn't have regular partners, and this big girl, Lena Sidoli, very buxom, more or less taught him by just pushing him round the floor. Aldo, who is not a lot taller than me, seemed to enjoy it thoroughly. When he felt confident enough he asked me to partner him and we got on famously and, very gradually, danced more and more together. It would be silly to say we were childhood sweethearts just because we had played together in the street; our mothers were great friends so we knew each other very well. There was no flash-of-lightning type falling in love; we just spent more and more time together and I secretly thought he looked just like Clark Gable in his dashing white-silk evening scarf.

We were all cinema crazy and went to the pictures twice a week if we could (they used to change the programmes twice weekly in those days) and you sat in the back row for a cuddle. Our heartthrobs were Tyrone Power, Don Ameche, Cesare Romero, Robert Taylor, Melvyn Douglas and, of course, Clark Gable. The girls all wanted to look like filmstars and we would spend hours looking at film magazines and poring over pictures of Maureen O'Hara, Olivia de Havilland, Alice Faye and Myrna Loy. Everyone wanted to look like them and I made dresses for my girlfriends so they could. Funny thing is I never wanted to *look* like a filmstar but, oh, how I wanted to dance like Ginger Rogers.

We also went to the music halls though they were called Variety by then. I think Collins on Islington Green was the last one to keep the title Music Hall. The Holborn Empire was nearby and the Islington Empire and we would go to see Max Miller, Larry Adler, Rob Wilton, Vera Lynn, Anne Shelton and Harry Roy and his Band. Very occasionally we would have a gin and orange cordial either at the interval or at a dance, just the one – it was all the boys could afford, and the days of women buying drinks for men like now were not even a twinkle in a barman's eye. Naturally the boys would escort us home even though the streets were safe. It would have been considered very improper to allow a girl to walk home alone and parents would have been so outraged the chap would never have darkened their doors again. We were all very well brought up to old-fashioned standards. I remember thinking it really rather odd that Aldo, who often escorted me home, did not always walk on the outside of the pavement. It was a long time before he overcame his shyness and confessed that he was deaf in his right ear and would not have been able to talk to me if he had swopped sides every time we crossed a road. It was a lovely life: sometimes a whole coachload of us would go down to Hastings for the day, and whoever organised the booking provided the picnic. We would sit on the cliffs with someone playing the accordion and have a sing-song; then it would either be a stroll along the beach with a swim or a trip to the funfair (and to this day I have never *quite* forgiven Aldo for ruining my stockings on the bumper cars). Then along came the war.

A whole group of us, including Aldo, had just returned from a week's holiday in Hastings; three girls all in one room, indeed all in one bed, the boys all together in another room; certainly no hanky-panky (can you imagine a pre-war seaside landlady allowing it even if it had crossed our minds?) but lots of giggles and confidences. It was a Saturday when we returned and we arranged to meet in Ted's Cafe after Mass. At eleven o'clock on the Sunday morning Neville Chamberlain announced over the wireless that we were at war with Germany and for the first time in my life I saw my father break down and cry; in my innocence I couldn't understand why. I had no idea what war meant. Of course I had seen pictures on *Movietone News* while waiting for the main feature film, but that all happened in places like China, a million miles away as far as I was concerned. So I went to Mass and on to Ted's Cafe to find out when the next school-hall dance was to be held. It was cancelled and the boys were already talking about enlisting, as I suppose they were in every town, city and village in Britain.

At first the war made little or no difference to our daily lives except that we were issued with pale-blue identity cards and gas masks that we had to carry everywhere with us. We also had to make blackout curtains for all the windows. Food was rationed but for families who had been brought up on hardship it made very little difference. There were sandbags outside important buildings and barrage balloons in the sky. The biggest impact on our young lives during the 'phoney' war was that the dance-halls stopped us wearing our long dresses in case we had to flee to an air-raid shelter.

Italy had not joined Hitler on 3 September, even though she had made an alliance with Germany in May 1939, so my two older brothers had no difficulty joining the army because they were British by birth. As far as we were concerned we were all in this together; it was a new bond with our neighbours, who outside our community were mostly English, and I couldn't understand why my parents were so apprehensive.

Slowly the younger generation learned; people of German extraction were being rounded up and interned, even those who had fled from Nazi Germany, and as France began to face defeat the Italians came under scrutiny. When, after Dunkirk, Mussolini declared war on Britain, on 10 June 1940, Winston Churchill's immediate reaction was, 'Collar the lot.' He meant us.

The police went to work that very night and arrested several hundred Italians all over the country; four days later over 1,500 had indeed been collared. Round our manor every Italian male aged between sixteen and sixty kept a bag packed in readiness for the dreaded knock on the door from the police. Over the next two weeks 4,000 people were arrested, among them some of the grandest names in West End catering – men who were renowned at the Ritz, the Savoy and Claridges – as well as humble waiters and owners of small cafés. Everyone was suspected of belonging to the Fascio Party.

As working-class families none of us in the Clerkenwell vicinity had felt the need of Mussolini's protection; it was more for the élitist professions in Britian, a bit like the Freemasons I suppose. Anyhow, anyone who had attended a Fascio dinner in the banqueting rooms in Charing Cross Road or donated to the party's funds was on the MI5 blacklist – and that included the poor people who paid their taxes on a tiny property in Italy from here. I shuddered when I recalled all of us marching past Dr Rampagna with our fists raised and our parade at the Edgware Sports Ground.

I shook even more when the knock came on our front door. They had come for Papa. I told them Papa was ill – which he was as the worry was slowly killing him – and that if they took him they would have to take me, too, to look after him. I was very indignant and told them that my two brothers were already in the army. They insisted on taking away our radio and I had to go down to the City Road police station to get permission to keep it. There I found two more friends, Ben and his brother Micki, two of the best waiters in town. They had been sitting there for hours and begged me to come back with a pack of cards, which I did. Then I went to their home and told their sisters and mum where they were – because that was part of the horror: the police wouldn't say where they were taking anyone; once they left their own front door there was no communication whatsoever.

By 24 June 27,200 people had been interned, scattered in camps all over Britain, fathers taken from wives and children, sons from parents. Not all were Italians. There were Germans, Austrians and Jews as well. Aliens they were called, and it touched us all. No wonder my father had cried the day war was declared. He could remember the 29,000 people who had been victims of internment during the First World War, and the smashed windows and hatred that accompanied it. We were luckier. Our English neighbours never shunned or distrusted us, they were kind and concerned, but the newspapers were horrible with constant references to 'the Fifth Column in our midst'.

Nobody knew what was happening. There were rumours that everyone was to be shipped off to the Isle of Man, which was miserable for their families but not frightening; they would be safe there. The government had other plans: the internees were to be deported to the colonies like convicts from the last century – and that was exactly how they were treated. We found out because the ship they were being transported on, the *Arandora Star*, one of the greatest pre-war luxury liners, was torpedoed within twenty-four hours of setting sail from Liverpool on 1 July, barely three weeks after Churchill had barked his order. Of the 712 Italian internees aboard 486 were lost, among them many grand and famous figures from the West End (Zangiacomi and Maggi from the Ritz, Zavattoni from the Savoy, Sovrani of the Normandie, Benini of the Hungaria), together with humble waiters, pastrycooks and barbers. Nimfa's sister's sweetheart was drowned and many of Aldo's chums.

It was a deep and terrible sorrow to be shared by us at home but it was even worse for the survivors; seven days later they were put on board the *Dunera* and once more set sail for Australia. Living conditions were so appalling, and the brutality from the military crew so disgusting, that Serefino Pini, a man who had owned a restaurant in St James's, attached his wedding ring to his private parts by a piece of wire so that it wouldn't be stolen by them. And they have to cheek to make jokes about the Italians being yellow.

When I was taking my sentimental wander round my old home patch I popped into see Mr Gazzano whose family have had a shop on Farringdon Road since 1901. He was interned in 1940 and told me that he had been allocated a ticket on the *Arandora Star* but gave it up to a man he knew whose sixteen-year-old son was sailing on it and who asked him to swop places so he could be with his boy. Father and son were both lost. Many of the men I was to work with later were also interned, among them Mr Bianchi and Mr Bossi's brother. Mr Polledri, who owned a little café in Floral Street and bought the Bar Italia from Mr Bianchi after the war, was physically dragged away from his wife and three-year-old son Nino (who now owns the place).

It happened so fast all because the War Office, the Home Office and the Foreign Office had their wires crossed; it was a bureaucratic cock-up that, thank God, Parliament was quick to recognise. By the end of August 1940 many of the utterly innocent internees were being released. I was able to fill in the background details to it all many years later from an excellent book by Peter and Leni Gillman entitled, in Churchill's immortal words, *Collar the Lot*.

The internees who were released early got home just

in time for the Blitz which began in September and it was in the generally tense atmosphere then prevailing that I proposed to Aldo. Perhaps proposed is the wrong word; I told him 'I think we should get married.' Aldo had been turned down at his army medical because of his perforated eardrum, a result of his early bouts of diphtheria and scarlet fever. He had joined the ARP (Air Raid Warning Patrol), so he was exempt from being interned, but his father, like many men of foreign extraction, was not allowed to go farther than five miles from home. This rule applied even if a man's workplace was ten miles from where he lived.

It was around this time that clothes rationing was introduced and the small fashion houses were forced to close down. Although by now I could fall back on a bit of home-sewing (12/6d for a dress, 7/6d for a skirt), I couldn't make ends meet because now there wasn't much material about and people didn't have the coupons. So through my friend Peggy Mann, who was the receptionist, I took a job as a cleaner to a doctor in Shaftesbury Avenue. I polished the brass plate outside, kept the place clean and sometimes delivered letters to Harley Street.

At the back of my mind I vaguely thought it was a bit odd that Dr Spencer-Lewis had no male patients, only posh girls with their mamas. Then one day Peggy told me the surgery was closing down. No reason was given and I was far too concerned about being out of work again to wonder, but I found out the next day when I opened the paper. Dr Spencer-Lewis had been arrested. I'd been working for an abortion clinic (an enterprise totally illegal at that time) and had been too naïve to know it.

My younger brother Mario had been evacuated to a

small mining village called Tamworth just outside Birmingham and when the nightly bombing started I managed to get compassionate permission for my parents to join him; poor Papa's nerves simply couldn't take the raids. Aldo and his sister moved in with me (and the remaining lodgers) and most weekends we would travel up to see them; oddly, despite the war, the trains ran regularly. We would walk back from Euston in the blackout, hiding in doorways if there was an air-raid warning.

It was on one of these visits that we told my parents that we wanted to get married. We planned a simple ceremony, no fuss. Mama was most indignant. Her only daughter was going to have a proper wedding, war or no war. Aldo had already bought me an engagement ring. We had gazed at it in the window of Samuels in Kings Cross for weeks till he could afford it. Nineteen guineas it cost, a lot of money in those days. Aldo was by now working on demolition sites with teams of the returned Italian internees clearing the bomb damage. It was hard and dirty work but somehow Aldo always managed to look elegant in his white silk scarf and trilby hat. Indeed, throughout the war everyone made an enormous effort to look clean and stylish. So we set about planning our wedding in the midst of absolute chaos.

It wasn't easy, material was both scarce and rationed, but Nimfa and I found some silver-and-white brocade at Debenham and Freebody's in Oxford Street. It wasn't enough for a long dress but when we found some silver-and-white lace in John Lewis Nimfa was able to design a combination of the two with a sweetheart neckline. The result was very pretty and, nearly fifty years later, I've still got it tucked away in a box upstairs. I bought my veil and head-dress from Bourne and

Hollingsworth. Mama gave me all her coupons so I made the bridesmaids' dresses out of fuchsia moiré silk – there were no synthetics then. Come to think of it I wonder if two of my customers today at L'Escargot, David and Elizabeth Emmanuel who designed Princess Diana's wedding dress, could have done better in the circumstances.

I ordered my flowers from Snows just down my road and again nearly fifty years later each Monday morning I collect the flowers for L'Escargot from the same family shop; that is the only day I don't come in by bus. I ordered my wedding cake from Buzzards in Oxford Street, famous for its cakes and confectionary, and the day before the wedding went along to collect it (no such luxuries as delivery vans while there was a petrol shortage). I was very excited but when I got to the place the whole area was cordoned off because the shop had been hit by a bomb the night before. I turned to the policeman guarding the barrier and wailed, 'My wedding cake, my wedding cake.' I told him I was getting married the following day. He must have had a kind heart for he assured me that only the shop had been hit and against orders let me through and directed me to a little alleyway at the side and down some steps to the bakery at the back. The staff were all there and so was my cake. They had intended to take it to the front shop that morning. They were as thrilled as I was that it was safe and they packed it carefully into two boxes which I triumphantly carried home on the bus.

And I've still got the top decoration although it took twenty-five years to come home. My friend Peggy Mann who had found me the job with Dr Spencer-Lewis came to the wedding and took the top layer of the cake away for safety because she was living in the country and it was a tradition that the top layer should be cut at the christening of the first child. Somehow we lost touch and Adriana's christening came and went with no cake. At last, Peggy came to visit me on my silver wedding anniversary, bringing with her the decoration (not the cake itself, thank heavens) displayed under a little glass dome she had found in Scotland. What a dear and thoughtful friend.

I am eternally grateful that Mama insisted on a proper wedding. It was very grand and took place at St Peter's Italian Church on 20 April 1941. It was only on that morning when I went downstairs to pick up the papers – funny to think of such normal things as newspaper boys delivering during a war, isn't it? – that I discovered that we were getting married on Hitler's birthday. If I could have changed the day there and then I would have. I was mortified. But we comforted our innocent selves with the thought that Hitler wouldn't send his bombers over on his birthday. How wrong we were.

My elder brother Romeo gave me away because Papa had had a fall in the garden a few days earlier – he was already very frail – and he had a nasty cut on his face. Papa didn't want to spoil my beautiful day in any way but he came to the reception at Reggiori's in Kings Cross, a gorgeous place with fountains and Edwardian tiling that a lot of Italians used for weddings. There was a family lunch and then all our younger friends joined us for the singing and dancing.

At nine o'clock the bombing began. Hitler had decided not to be sentimental about his birthday or my wedding day so the restaurant had to close. We all trooped, a great procession of us, musicians and all, and with me still in my wedding dress, up the Pentonville Road to carry on the party at home while the bombs dropped all round. Then at two in the morning Aldo and I walked to a borrowed flat nearby where we honeymooned for a week.

We were to live a small flat Mama had given us on the first floor of her house; it was just a bedroom and a kitchen really (the bedroom is now our sitting room). Mama was adamant that I had a kitchen on my own, saying firmly that no two women could share one. She was also very firm about privacy: 'If you have an argument, stay in your own place,' she would say. 'Come down and see us when you are happy.' Aldo and I did have a few arguments at first – he didn't like living with my parents and wanted us to get a place of our own – but I couldn't leave them, Papa was too ill. Anyhow we are still living in the same place so you can see who won.

Meanwhile the bombing became very heavy and we had several narrow escapes. There was a particularly nasty type of bomb called a Molotov Basket which when it landed sent small fire-bombs scattering in all directions. One hit our back bedroom and two of Mama's lodgers came hurtling down the stairs yelling that the house was on fire. We all grabbed buckets of water and raced up and down the stairs. Aldo put a wet handkerchief over his face and at last managed to put the fires out, but he inhaled a lot of smoke and has been susceptible to bronchitis ever since. While all this was going on, six highly explosive devices dropped in the streets round us; one landed on the house at the bottom of our garden and I was nearly blown through the window. By then the house next door was fully ablaze and we all had to get out. Aldo piggy-backed Papa and we all ran towards the Angel tube station. The bombs were coming down at the rate of one a minute that night and as we hurried along the local Protestant priest saw us and offered us sanctuary in his presbytery – which was kind because we were not his parishioners. Somehow we felt we would be safer at the Angel and continued to make our way there; just as well – the presbytery got a direct hit.

It was a fearsome night and the tube station was so jam-packed there wasn't even room for people to sit, let alone lie down. We all stood all night desperately hoping our house was safe. Nobody ever knew if they would have a home to go to in the morning. The All Clear sounded at six in the morning and while I got the family together Aldo ran ahead to see if our house was still standing. He wanted to spare my parents the horror if necessary. Then the warning sounded again and we were stuck underground for another hour, with me praying all the time for Aldo's safety – we had only been married three weeks. The All Clear sounded again and when we got up to the street there was no sign of Aldo. I was beside myself with anxiety. The house next door was burnt to a cinder but ours still stood. The heat was almost unbearable but I charged in calling for Aldo. When he answered from the basement I screamed back, 'Where the hell have you been?'

'I've been making a cup of tea. I thought you'd all need one,' he said mildly and I didn't know whether to laugh or cry.

Out at the back was the most terrible scene, like an evil Christmas. All the trees were covered in white ash and festooned with people's belonging – clothes, furniture, pictures. The three little girls from the house at the bottom of our garden were orphaned that night. It was shocking.

We didn't go to the tube every night; sometimes we

all slept on the floor in the basement. It was impossible to estimate just how close each raid was going to come. The bombing seemed uncomfortably close one evening and we thought of taking shelter in Dame Alice Owen's School but decided in the end to stay put. To our dismay the school suffered a direct hit, taking with it two whole families I had grown up with. The raids went on throughout the war, though sometimes there were lulls for a time. I remember quite late on, when I was working in Soho again, I was coming home for my afternoon break when the siren went; we were near the Angel but the buses stopped automatically when the air-raid warning went off and this young girl just dumped the baby she had been carrying in my lap, leapt off the bus and started running. I was so surprised I just sat there holding it. The bus started up again and I got off at the Angel stop, ran after her and caught up with her by the entrance. Poor thing, she was so confused and panicked that she hardly knew what she was doing. It was a bad time for everybody's nerves.

Despite all that was happening, Aldo and I still went dancing whenever we could – sometimes locally and sometimes at the Royal Opera House which had been turned into a dance-hall. In fact we got into the finals of a dance competition there, which was very exciting; then I found out I was pregnant and that was the end of that.

There wasn't a great deal more information about for expectant mums then than there had been when I was a kid. The general attitude was that it was enough for you to know that it came out the same way it went in. Adriana was born during the bombing in the very cold winter of 1943, and as there was a coal shortage our neighbours all came round with bucketsful as gifts. We had no phone so Aldo had to run to the clinic to get the midwife. She set off on her bike but Aldo was home before her. She sat by the fire and got on with her knitting and when I asked her how much more of this I would have to endure she just looked at me and said, 'There's worse to come.' What a contrast to the cosseting and guidance women receive now.

View of Eyre Street Hill where I was born

Mama and Papa, Rosina and Luigi Maestri

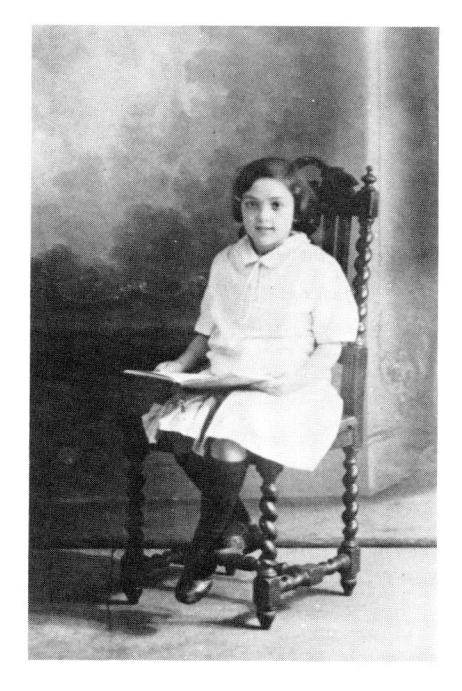

Myself aged nine

Sweet sixteen

Aged nineteen, in a hat

My wedding day

The children from Clerkenwell on holiday at Felixstowe

Early view of Frith Street

Bianchi's and the Bar Italia
in the thirties

Benjamino Gigli singing with the choir of St Peter's Italian Church

The Italian Procession, 1937 (*Times Newspapers Limited*)

With husband Aldo and daughter Adriana

Football-club outing

Outside the Café Bleu, in the thirties

Accordion player and singing waiter at the Café Bleu

Four

Adriana was about a year old when a friend mentioned there was a job as a waitress coming up at the Café Bleu in Old Compton Street. We were, as ever, hard up. Aldo was working in a factory making plaster statuettes. I checked with the family and Mama said she would look after the baby, so I went to see the owner, Mr Bossi. Even though I told him I had no experience in the job he was so short-staffed he let me start the following Monday. Mind you he wasn't taking much of a risk as I received no wages and was expected to survive on the tips I received. In spite of this he was a kind boss and at the end of the first day he told me he couldn't believe I had never done the job before.

Waitresses were a wartime innovation in Soho. There were, of course, the 'nippies' in Lyons teashops but in general serving at tables had always been a man's job; now there was a manpower shortage and we were welcome and treated with great respect. It was hard work. There were six of us and we did a roster of six days a week, each of us having one Sunday in six free. I made our uniforms, which were royal-blue pinafore frocks worn over crisp white blouses – though how I found the time, what with dashing home each afternoon to put the baby to bed, I can't imagine.

The Café Bleu was a pretty restaurant with royal-blue tiles outside, glass shell-shaped wall-lights, spotless white tablecloths and bentwood chairs. There were sixteen tables and Victor Berlemont, the father of Gaston who ran the York Minster (always known locally as the French Pub) in Dean Street, would send the visiting servicemen round to us so we were always busy – but it was fun, too. They were relaxing on leave and we did all we could to help them enjoy themselves. We didn't have a licence but we would run across the road to the Helvetia (now the Soho Brasserie) to fetch great jugs of beer – never mind if it was raining or snowing, it was part of our job. Sometimes a customer would want wine and we'd get that from the Algerian Wine Stores at seven shillings a bottle.

Of course there was a severe meat shortage so we mostly served minestrone, vegetable ravioli or mounds of spaghetti. Berwick Street market was open right through the war so there was no shortage of vegetables. Sometimes the American GIs would demand meatballs with their spaghetti and I would tell them that since they didn't send us any meat, only Spam, that's all they would get. I remember it was called Escalope Bruxelles with Spaghetti, very grand for a couple of slices of Spam dipped in reconstituted egg powder and breadcrumbs, then fried. But they were nice boys. Quite a few were of Italian extraction, though they couldn't speak the language, and when they found out I had a little girl they would bring cans of orange juice and bars of chocolate for her from their PX. Since most of the shops around were Italian-owned and run by mothers and daughters there was a certain amount of fraternisation. Several of the girls ended up as GI Brides. I even saw one I knew on a television programme about them years later.

Early in the war some French sailors had rescued a

cat from a bombsite and brought her to the café to be looked after. She was a beautiful big black cat and she would lounge in the window all day. Her name was Zuzu and she became a symbol of home for them all when they came on leave.

It was around this time I first learned about homosexuals, though we didn't call them that in those days; I think we probably muttered 'queers' or 'poofs' in our ignorance. The Helvetia was their hang-out and when it closed at two in the afternoon they came to the Café Bleu to eat. It wasn't a promiscuous place but they were invariably in pairs and I suppose I must have thought it strange to see men going about as couples. I was used to seeing the lads all hang out together but not as twosomes, so I probably mentioned it to one of the girls and she explained. It's so long ago and attitudes have changed so much it's difficult to remember how innocent those times were.

Still, we all knew the ladies of the street. They were so beautifully dressed with their sheer black silk stockings and high-heeled shoes and they wore little silver-fox tails over their shoulders. They each had their own pitch, which they would stroll up and down, and they all rented rooms above shops in the area which they only used during the day. Sometimes they would come to the café with a client, usually officer-class, and sometimes they would come in with their maids, incredibly respectable-looking women; if you saw them on a bus you'd never guess their role in life. Even so we always treated them with equal respect; it's not in the Soho mentality to pass judgement on people for the way they earn their living.

The Café Bleu attracted all kinds of people as Soho always has – artists, writers, actors and mysteries. Mostly, unless they made the newspapers either by becoming famous or infamous, I knew nothing about my customers except the food they liked. I did recognise Michael Redgrave and Derek and Terence de Marney because they were filmstars, but fame was not important because we were all of us more concerned with whether we would be alive tomorrow. As usual, I'd go to work by bus but if we had to close the restaurant early because of the bombing, I'd go home by tube. Mr Bossi and Mr Paccini the manager, who had been interned with Mr Bossi's brother, would take it in turns to stay on the premises overnight for firewatch duty. When the raid was bad the locals (and there were lots of people living in Soho then) would head for the underground at Leicester Square. Everybody had their own pitch and it was quite safe to leave a sleeping bag or blankets down there. People would play cards or have a sing-song and we would all greet each other and say 'See you tomorrow' when we dispersed – in a ritual of good luck. Throughout the war the trains ran on time, much more efficiently than now. At the Angel station people slept on the narrow platform with trains passing by on either side. It was a nightmare but nobody complained; I suppose we just got used to it.

On D-Day in June 1944 when the Allied Forces invaded France a whole crowd of French soldiers and sailors came roaring into the Café Bleu to celebrate. They grabbed all the waitresses and the chefs too and took us dancing in the street; any customers just had to wait till the exuberance had died down. It was fun and a welcome relief. We all thought the end was in sight but although the tide was turning we still had almost another year of bombing, doodle-bugs and V–2s to go through before VE-Day in May 1945. Papa never saw the end of the war, he died in August 1944. Now, although Norman Balon, the proprietor of the Coach & Horses in Greek Street (made so famous by Jeffrey Bernard) remembers Mr Bossi as a lunatic, I would take issue with him; Mr Bossi may have been a lunatic but he just was a loving lunatic who perhaps liked his gin and Noilly Prat a trifle too much. The first thing he did when he heard of Papa's death was to ask how we were off financially and whether we could afford a decent funeral. It was sweet but unnecessary, Mama being the kind of woman whose pride and independence made sure that such inevitabilities were saved for carefully.

Incidentally, Jeffrey Bernard and Bruce his brother, both incredibly handsome boys, frequented the Café Bleu in the late forties. I sometimes wonder what they would have thought if they had been aware of the identity of the leader of an earlier group of regulars. This was Quentin Joyce, the brother of William Joyce, the man who was known throughout the war as Lord Haw-Haw, an Establishment Englishman who broadcast propaganda for Hitler. His 'Jairmany calling, Jairmany calling' was mocked by every comic in the land. Soon after the war ended he was captured by the British, tried at the Old Bailey and found guilty of treason. One day Quentin Joyce and his friend, the son of Admiral Dorville, came in rather late and agitated and said I must serve them lunch because they had just come from their vigil outside the prison where Quentin's brother had been hanged that morning. It was very chilling; I know I wouldn't have felt like eating if it had been one of my brothers but they all appeared quite calm and tucked in. At Christmas they left me a little note on the back of a

Café Bleu good-wishes card saying, 'To Elena, the Mighty Atom'. None of us had even heard of the atom bomb then but we were later to be made horribly aware of its existence and the devastation it could wreak. I wasn't too flattered by the implication, but I do still have the card.

The end of the war was a wonderful relief from the prospect of being killed in our beds, or anywhere else for that matter, but it didn't alter the fact that there was still a severe food shortage. Our customers would peer suspiciously at the occasional meat dish and ask, a bit querulously, whether it was horse-flesh. I used to say I didn't know. There was a horse-meat shop in Frith Street and I regularly went to Smithfield, too, to buy it for my family and friends. I knew the value of plenty of protein and wasn't repelled by the thought of eating horse-meat. Before the war Mama had sent me to an aunt in Italy because I was so under-weight and scraggy, and my auntie had fed me horse-flesh to build me up. I suppose she was what you would describe as a peasant and peasants have never been choosy when it comes to survival. I must have inherited something from my background and I made my family delicious and nourishing meals of spaghetti Bolognaise, meatballs and stew without a qualm. I got stopped by the police once returning from Smithfield; they were very hot on black-marketing and I did look a bit laden in a world where most people could carry home their week's ration balanced on their little finger. They wanted to know what was in my shopping bags; I told them and showed them, explaining to them that horse-meat was perfectly legal, something they didn't even know, so they let me go. I was glad they hadn't stopped me on another day because I often bought black-market eggs in Soho for one shilling each and sometimes managed to get hold of black-market sugar too.

The end of the war also brought about a complete repudiation of Churchill's 'Collar the Lot' dictum. The first Italian touring company to come to London was the San Carlos Opera House from Milan, who put on a season at the Cambridge Theatre at Seven Dials. Naturally they came to Soho to eat and found the Café Bleu; that is how I met two of the singers, one a tenor and the other a massive great bear of a man, the baritone.

They commandeered me as soon as they discovered I spoke both Italian and English; they were having a row with Equity, the Actors' Union about which I knew nothing, over their contract and refused to sing more than three times a week – something which I believe they would never be required to do today. So off I went with them to translate their problems. It was all quite bewildering for me, but we won. They then informed me that they must have red meat to keep up their strength for singing; so once again it was back to Smithfield to purchase horse-meat which they readily accepted – great big steaks daily. In exchange they gave me tickets for the opera which was very exciting – my first introduction to the joys of *Tosca* and *The Barber of Seville*. I have to admit that I was a bit embarrassed when they indicated from the stage that they knew where I was sitting, but it was exhilarating too, somehow a symbol that the war was at long last over.

Meanwhile the black market flourished in post-war Soho; a suitcase full of treasured nylons could do a lot for a chap in those days – or a 'spiv' as he was called. Soho's underbelly has always been active and most of us who worked, one way or another, round the manor knew each other from schooldays. As well as the prostitutes on the street there were some pretty lively bookies who also had their own patches.

I knew all about bookies from my childhood in Clerkenwell where every family left the front door open automatically on their account. One day, when for some reason or other Papa was not at work, there was a tremendous commotion in the passage, a great clattering of boots and the noise of the copper boiler in the yard going flying. 'What's that?' yelled Papa.

'It will just be one of the bookies,' replied Mama calmly.

When a bookie was chased by the police, he dived through any front door, out through the back and over the wall into the next street. The police couldn't enter a house so he got away; it was a procedure everyone took for granted.

My 'Aunt' Connie, the one who lived across the road and made wonderful pizzas, was a terrible gambler. She swore like a trooper, too, and used to send her daughter out with the betting slips. One day I was at their house and Mary was having a piano lesson so she bullied me into going to the corner with her bet. I was terrified the police would catch me – though, of course, I knew who the 'runner' (the man who took illegal bets) was. I looked all round, then shoved the bet into his hand and ran home like the wind. Mama was furious and shocked Aunt Connie could have done such a thing (though she never turned a hair when the bookies used her back yard as an escape route). But I imagine one look at my scared face was enough to reassure her that I was not going to follow in Aunt Connie's footsteps. And indeed I very seldom even swear, perhaps the occasional 'bloody', and I certainly don't gamble. I've worked hard for every penny – still, it takes all sorts.

Albert Dimes was a bookie in Frith Street before off-course betting was made legal in 1958. I knew him well because I had been to school with his younger sister (Albert's real name was Dimeo). In the forties and fifties the rivalry between the bookies was extremely serious, so serious that they would not use the same café. This was why Jack Spot, whose pitch was Dean Street, never came into the Café Bleu as Albert was a regular.

In 1947, I took my first holiday since that week before the war in Hastings. My friend Mary and I went to Lugano in Switzerland; Aldo couldn't get away but thought I needed a break. Post-war Britain was still very austere. You could only take £50 out of the country so every penny had to be watched – but we had fun. We decided to take the train to Milan to visit my aunt for a day; we could just afford the fare. With the typical generosity of the Italians she insisted that we stay for a couple of days as she wanted to catch up on family news. It was an offer we couldn't refuse, as they say, but it was embarrassing. Italy was very poor and to accept hospitality meant putting a strain on the family. Fortunately the Italian-Soho connection came in handy. I met a Mr Sidoli, a familiar figure from the market in London, and borrowed enough lira to pay our way knowing I would be able to repay the debt when I got home. Less fortunately I ran into another friend from Clerkenwell, Winnie Driver. It didn't seem unfortunate at first. She was full of the good news about one of her two sisters – the three of them had been the most beautiful girls on the block. Her sister had married a very wealthy man, was living in Belgravia and often sent money home. A few weeks after our return I opened the paper and saw this sister's picture; she had been found murdered in Wardour Street. It was revealed that she was known locally as Black Rita, a prostitute. It must all have come as a terrible shock to her family.

I had a terrible shock, too, one morning when I came into work as usual: the Café Bleu had burnt down in the night. Apparently the fire had been sparked off by an electrical fault under the stairs. Poor Mr Bossi was distraught. When I thought of all those years during the war he and Mr Paccini had stayed on the premises to defend the place against the German bombs, it didn't seem fair. I was a bit distraught myself – about my own future.

In the event, it was back to the old sewing machine. Mama's death in 1948 had been devastating both for me and for Adriana; Nonna, as she called her, had been everything to her. In a curious way, sitting using Mama's machine was comforting to me. It was an old treadle-worked Singer that Papa had given her for their first wedding anniversary in 1911. I still have it and still use it. Aldo has often offered to buy me an electric machine but I can see no point when I am happy and content with the one I have and for me it is my connection with my past.

It is also Mama and Papa's connection with the future generation. A couple of Christmases ago Matthew, one of my grandchildren, announced that he wanted a toy elephant as his present. Now I am nothing if not an indulgent grandmama (or Nonna, as *I* am now called in the Italian tradition) so off I trotted to John Lewis, my old haunt, and to the toy department. Well, I know I see people spending the kind of money for a meal at

L'Escargot that would have kept a family for a year when I was young, that's just part of inflation. But eighty-six quid for a toy? I couldn't do it. I was really shocked, thinking that that amount of money should be spent on clothes (shades of my own early Christmases I suppose). I went down to the pattern department and there I found a package for making an elephant complete with material, eyes and stuffing all for under a fiver. I rushed home to Mama's sewing machine and spent a couple of happy hours assembling it and my pleasure was reflected in Matthew's joy when he opened his present. Mama would have approved.

I keep the machine in an upstairs room and over it I drape one of Mama's pillow overlays – not a pillowcase, you understand, but the beautifully hand-embroidered, lace-edged cloth she used to cover each pillow during the daytime. We may have lived in what would now be considered hovels but oh, how proud Italian women were of their linen and lace, and how it has endured. I still have some of her clothes too – cotton bodices with crochet edges, an ecru silk blouse trimmed with exquisite hand-wrought fine lace which she used for best, and a tiny black silk cummerbund. I marvel when I look at the stitching round the hooks and eyes – so tiny, so fine and so strong – and remember that when I was young nobody wore glasses.

Keeping Mama's things isn't the least bit morbid because I happen, by nature, to be the most terrible hoarder! I have boxes and boxes of cuttings from newspapers and magazines about the customers who have become my friends, and albums full of pictures of them. I cannot bear to throw away a single card, letter or note. It seems to me that when people bother to think of you from the other side of the world their kindness is worth treasuring. I wouldn't part with any signed book either.

Five

After the fire closed down the Café Bleu, Mr Paccini the manager (who had been interned with Mr Bianchi) joined Bianchi's and I started sewing again. Then one day I phoned Mrs Paccini for a chat and she told me they were short-staffed and suggested I give Mr Paccini a call. I rang him on Friday and started on the Monday. This was in 1951.

It was a happy restaurant which Mr Bianchi had started in ground-floor premises in 1928 with very simple food. Later he expanded on to the first floor and offered a more varied menu. The two rooms were light and airy with big windows and large mirrors. Although it was quite simple it was already very popular among theatrical people and artists and writers, so there were lots of posters and signed photographs on the walls.

It was here that I began many life-long friendships, often over three generations. In the fifties there was still a certain amount of formality in relationships but, although the class barrier still functioned elsewhere, there was little or no snobbery in Soho. People dressed formally too; ladies always wore hats and gloves and gentlemen would not have dreamed of removing their jackets in a restaurant. I remember people like Michael Wilding and Margaret Leighton lunching at Bianchi's; it would never have occurred to him not to rise to his feet when she left the table to powder her nose (ladies did nothing so vulgar as to go to the loo in those days) and on her return. They were a beautiful couple, so elegant and so obviously fond of each other. Another great couple was Dame Sybil Thorndike and her husband Lewis Casson. Her voice was wonderful to hear and very carrying. One day they were having lunch with some friends and while she was enjoying herself he was getting anxious about an appointment and kept on about them catching the tube. 'My dears,' said Dame Sybil, in ringing tones, 'he still thinks we can't afford a cab!' However, it was said with such an indulgent smile nobody could have been offended.

I think at first I was a bit overawed by all these great names but I made my breakthrough with Bud Abbott and Lou Costello when they were appearing at the Palladium. For some reason I was looking out of the window when they arrived and they glanced up and said, 'Look there's a boid looking at us.' When they got upstairs, 'There's our boid,' was their greeting. I took their order and arrived at the table with two bowls of soup. 'That's his,' 'No that's his, that's mine!' They kept this up while I dithered from one to the other. Every time I tried to place the bowls they changed their minds. Eventually I got fed up and told them that if they went on like this they would each have a bowl of soup in their laps. They meekly apologised. This is how I learnt to control my customers, a lesson that has stood me in good stead on many occasions over the last thirty years.

Mind you, some were quite impossible and I had to learn to cope with that, too. When Maria Callas swept in wearing a full-length mink coat I politely offered to hang it up, but she was not going to be parted from it and insisted that it remained draped over the back of her chair. No amount of reassurance from either Mr Bianchi or myself that we would guard it with our lives made any difference so I had to try not to trip over the wretched thing all through lunch. I suppose it *was* very precious, mink was both rare and expensive in the fifties. Another piece of arrogance I found hard to swallow was when Lili Palmer sailed in with an imperious wave of her hand, saying, 'I've left a taxi downstairs, pay it for me.' I nipped down to discover how much it was and found she owed the man two pounds, a lot of money to me. Fortunately she was lunching with a regular customer and when I told him of this slight problem he said expansively, 'Just put it on the bill.' Not the sort of behaviour I approved of; to me each person that comes through the door is a human being, famous or not, and I like to treat them as such, but I expect to be treated in the same way.

When I had been at Bianchi's for about a year I fell pregnant again, a fact I tried hard to disguise by wearing a roll-on, but it was impossible for long. I told Mr Bianchi that I would have to leave and he asked me to stay on a bit longer as he was going on his annual holiday with his family to Italy for three weeks. In the event he stayed over in Milan for two months and I was getting quite plump by them. The first person to comment was Marguerite Bourke-Sheridan, a retired opera singer, an enormous woman, all chiffon scarves and hats who became hysterical if anyone sneezed or coughed within her hearing. The fact that she no longer performed made no difference, she was very protective of her voice. She never booked but expected her table, number 22, to be free at all times. If it wasn't she would treat the occupant to a shrivelling, disdainful look. Mind you, perhaps she was entitled to; it was at that table the great Gigli had sung a duet with her before the war.

'Elena, you are putting on weight, it must be gluttony,' she announced one day in a voice that could be heard all over Soho and had once reached the gods in Covent Garden.

'No, Miss Sheridan, I'm not eating too much, I'm pregnant.'

She was shocked. 'I told you not to trust men,' she commented.

I think she had forgotten that I was a married woman and already had a daughter aged nine. She went on about how I should have nothing more to do with men. I had a strong feeling that it was a long time since she had had anything to do with men herself.

The other person to notice was Sergeant Davies, who was Sir Winston Churchill's personal bodyguard. He was a very friendly man. One day when he made a joke I reached out to give him a playful push and my hand came up against the holster under his arm. I didn't say a word. He was quite direct about my own bulge and said to me, 'Elena, no point in trying to hide it, it's about time you gave up work, if you don't you'll be having it here.' So as soon as Mr Bianchi returned I took his advice and Louie was born on 18 January 1953.

Louie was just six months old when Mr Paccini rang me to ask if I could help him out while his waitresses took their summer holidays; three girls were taking two weeks each. I consulted Aldo and the family and my mother-in-law offered to look after the baby and Adriana. On the Monday I began probably the longest six weeks in recorded history; thirty years in fact. Thirty years of getting to know some of the most interesting, extraordinary, funny, talented, kind, outrageous and emotional people in the world.

At the beginning I didn't know many people unless they were famous like Tony Britten, who held all his first-night and last-night parties at Bianchi's. When I first met him he was starring in *Cactus Flower* with Margaret Leighton; their last-night party went on till four in the morning. It was the beginning of a life-long friendship. On the first night of *The Dame of Sark* the restaurant was filled with people who had been to see the play, and when Tony walked in everyone stood up to applaud him. He did a piece in German from the play and for a moment seemed to become a German officer; there was more clapping and then he turned and smiled and was my friend again.

Working long hours and raising a family I didn't have time to go to the cinema, and getting home in the afternoons to give the family their supper, I barely had time to glance at the papers. One day my friend Toni Dalli walked in with a friend of his saying they had been to a football match at Fulham and his guest's car had been impounded. Would I ring the police and find out where it had been taken? I made a note of the name and car number without a glimmer of recognition; the police thought I was having them on. I couldn't see the point of the joke and kept repeating that the man was a friend of one of my customers. It was only when I put the phone down that my staff, who were all grinning at me, told me that the name I had given, Sean Connery, was that of the biggest filmstar in the West End, James Bond himself. He still teases me about that incident.

As time went by and I became a fixture the people

who had become my friends would introduce me to their friends, often insisting that I use their Christian names. I had a good memory for faces and people's likes and dislikes in food, and I enjoyed looking after them. I never became over-familiar and certainly didn't eavesdrop on their conversations, but we would have a laugh towards the coffee stage of the meal. It was all so friendly and relaxed, which made it all the more surprising when I found out just who they were. I had served David Cornwell for years before I discovered when going past a bookshop and seeing his picture in the window that he was John Le Carré. The first time he came in, he was about seventeen and terribly shy. He told me later that it was his very first date with his very first girlfriend and that he had never played host in a restaurant before – no wonder he looked so nervous. He also reminds me that I helped him through the menu without in any way diminishing the very shaky manly pride of a young lad from the suburbs. I can't really claim credit for the success of the evening but he did marry the young lady and they were together for fifteen years. He still visits me at L'Escargot with his second wife, Anne, and is as charming as the boy I first met, despite the fact he is now world-famous.

People mostly paid by cash as there were no credit cards in those days, not even cheque cards. Once when Derek Mitchell offered me a cheque I asked him to put his address on the back which was the usual practice. He wrote 'Ten Downing Street' and I thought he was pulling my leg when I read it; I marched straight back to the table from the cash desk and demanded, 'What's all this?' He smiled and said, 'But I'm Harold Wilson's press secretary. Didn't you know, Elena?'

I tried apologising but he wouldn't have it. Still, I got

a small revenge for feeling foolish; I told him he'd better be careful as he was sitting in the hot seat, the one that Mandy Rice-Davies had sat in one day while the Old Bailey trial was going on. She had come in with Pelham Pound, a journalist, and while you didn't often see Bianchi's customers in a flutter she did cause quite a stir. The following day Pelham Pound came in with Stephen Ward and I still wonder if John Hurt, who was already a regular and was to play Ward so sympathetically twenty-five years later, was in the restaurant that day.

Tables 12 and 15 were favourites with politicians and political journalists; they were tucked into the corners of the big room, ideal for discreet conversations. Antony Sampson and Nora Beloff of the *Observer* were regulars and so was a man I thought was a doctor as he always told me he was on call. He still wore his demob suit, his grandfather's mac and if I remember rightly his grandfather's shoes too. One day he was sitting alone reading the papers which were full of speculation about Rab Butler becoming the next Prime Minister when, to be conversational, I asked his opinion. 'Elena, you mustn't ask me such questions,' was his reply. I said, 'Why? Aren't you interested in politics?' He looked at me a bit oddly and asked if I knew what he did and I told him of course I did, he was a doctor and that was why he was always on call. He thought this very funny. He was in fact Harold Macmillan's private secretary. Soon after I saw his photograph in the paper going to the Palace with Macmillan when he went to offer his resignation. Later, my dear 'doctor' friend became Sir Timothy Bligh.

Alas, my innocence or ignorance of the status of people in high places still did not improve. An artist introduced his cousin James Orr to Bianchi's and he soon became a regular, a very straightforward man of the old school, always interested in other people's lives. He loved to get me talking about Soho and my own background. When President de Gaulle paid a state visit to London there was a gala performance in his honour at the Royal Opera House. As I hadn't been invited I was doing my usual work of serving my customers when the buzzer from Mr Bianchi's office sounded three times in the servery. This was the signal to come upstairs immediately. I rushed up to the office to find Mr Bianchi pointing at his little black-and-white television set in great excitement. 'Look, Elena, look, there's that man who comes into the restaurant and always talks to you. look, he's sitting in the royal box right beside the Queen.' We were both thrilled and wondered what he was doing there. When he came in next time I told him I'd seen him on the box, and that's when he told me he was Prince Philip's private secretary. Being a keen racing man he often accompanied the Queen to the races and when one day Albert Dimes came in he called me over to ask about him. 'Who is that young man there? I often see him at the races and he gives me lots of tips.' Well he would, wouldn't he? I should have said, seeing where he was sitting, but I just told him he was the older brother of someone I had been to school with.

I didn't mention the day a few years before when I had passed Albert on my way to work; he was sitting on the mudguard of a car on the corner of Frith Street, and as I turned into the doorway I heard a commotion behind me and saw men running in all directions. It was the day Albert Dimes and Jack Spot had their famous knifing fight which ended up in the vegetable shop on the corner of Greek Street (now a dress shop). The lady who ran it, Mrs Hyman, hit them both on the head with her heavy brass weighing pan which was funny and brave, although they wouldn't have touched her. They both ended up in hospital and the papers made a great fuss about the violence on the streets of Soho, the gang warfare, and the publicity probably helped to hurry the change in the law that made betting shops legal in 1958.

James Orr's great chum was Bill Heseltine who also worked at Buckingham Palace in the press office and later became the Queen's press secretary. He was a good-humoured Australian who was well liked by all the journalists; he had a wife and two children so we often talked about our families – it would never have occurred to me to mention his work. He went back to Australia for a couple of years but he didn't forget me. Sir Richard Colville, who was press secretary to the Queen at the time, came in on his return from a royal tour of Australia with a package and a letter: 'This was put on the Queen's flight for you,' he told me. Inside was a little koala bear and a sweet letter saying, 'Please reserve a seat for me when I come back.' It was Sir Richard who told me that Bill would be back to take over his job when he retired. When the time came he returned to England and on the great day of the celebration lunch I carefully folded my koala bear inside a cone-shaped napkin. It was wonderful to see him again – and his face when he lifted the napkin was a treat.

Many years later when I was in hospital for a check-up my Buck House group, as I used to call them, came in to find me missing, something so rare they asked what had happened to me. Late that evening when we were sitting around in the ward talking (by a curious coincidence two of my old schoolfriends were in for the same thing), a nurse came in with a brown-paper parcel which had just been hand-delivered. I thought it must be something I had asked Aldo to fetch for me but the nurse said, 'Who are you, Mrs Salvoni? What do you do?'

'I'm a waitress,' I told her.

'At Buckingham Palace?' she asked.

'No, why?'

'This parcel has the Queen's stamp on it.'

And so it did, a great purple ER. Inside was a lovely pink bed-jacket – a present from James Orr, Sir Richard Colville, Bill Heseltine and Miss Hawkins who also worked in the press office. Everyone was so excited they started to snatch bits of the brown paper but I managed to rescue the stamped bit and it is still one of my treasured souvenirs.

Another set of distinguished people formed themselves into the Cranium Club, a fellowship of professors and experts who used to meet about every three months at L'Escargot. Among the members were Sir William Coldstream, Sir Lawrence Gowing, Professor Freddie Ayer, Sir Isaiah Berlin, Solly Zuckerman, Sir Anthony Blunt and Stephen Spender, who still comes in, of course. They would book ahead and order a set meal and talk and talk. I don't know what they talked about because it would have been far above my head, and in any case I was far too busy serving their food. But they were all charming, Bill Coldstream especially. At the end of the meal they would each count out their share of the bill. They could not have been poor by any means but perhaps this was a leftover from their student days.

I suppose the revelation that Sir Anthony Blunt was a spy must have been as much of a shock to them as the defection of Burgess and Maclean had been to me. Donald Maclean and his wife Melinda had lunched at

Bianchi's two days before it happened and had appeared totally relaxed and at ease, not a hint of anxiety about them. Usually I'm pretty good at catching on to people's emotional states. I remember when two certain young couples came in one evening I said to Mary, one of the waitresses, 'This lot are up to some kind of mischief.' I don't know how I knew, they were very happy and well-behaved, but it was no surprise to read in the evening papers that James Goldsmith and Isobel Patino had eloped.

Six

Soho, being the place it is will always attract monsters, hangers-on and layabouts as well as those struggling to survive at the beginning of their careers or having a rough time halfway through. Many of my customers have gone through a bad patch either financially or emotionally. Many's the time I've loaded the tables with extra bread rolls and butter for young dancers and actors coming in late, very hungry and hard-up. They've all gone on to do well and I am happy that I could help them when they were starting out.

But I'm afraid I don't feel as charitable about the monsters and hangers-on. The strangest part is that the ones with the permanently empty pockets are the most arrogant and ill-mannered. Gerald Hamilton, who was said to be the model for Mr Norris in Christopher Isherwood's novel *Mr Norris Changes Trains*, was a revolting specimen in his attitude to life (which I read about later in the *Sunday Dispatch*) and his behaviour at the table. He slobbered over his food in the most disgusting manner and how anyone could sit opposite him and pay for the privilege I could never understand – but he certainly never paid for himself. We used to call him '*Barooza*' which is Italian slang for 'the dribbling one'.

I was never too pleased to see Tambimuttu either; he would arrive with his entourage, demanding tables be arranged to suit his party and showing no consideration for the other customers. I'm afraid he cut no ice with me, even though he often declared he was a prince in his own country, Ceylon. He had published poetry magazines in the forties, apparently good ones though he never paid his contributors. He never paid his bill either; whoever he had gathered up from one of the local pubs shared that honour and I must admit they seemed a forbearing lot. There was never any argument. However, his charm was lost on me. I suppose he was eccentric but the day he came in with a complete stranger saying that he wanted the whole room for the launch of some magazine and proceeded to put leaflets on the tables was really too much. The stranger was just as mad. He gave me a cheque for £250, to be cashed the following week, and said it would bring me great fortune. I saw that it was a Lloyds Bank cheque made out to Lloyds Bank. They must have thought I was as daft as they were. I let them have one table and made them pay cash. That was the last I saw of them.

There was another so-called prince (there were a lot of dubious titles around in the fifties) and this one put his feet on the table. I asked him to remove them and, when he refused, I told him to leave – very quietly, so as not to upset the other customers. He leapt up in a furry and smashed the fruit-stand. I managed to get him out but I would love to have hit him with that fruit-stand – and I don't often lose my temper.

Another absolute madman was Dennis Shaw, known as Den-Den, a man who could empty a pub quicker than 'Time, gentlemen, please'. He was vast, over six-foot tall, with a coarse face covered in large warts; a small-part film actor, he seemed to spend more time in the police cells than in front of the cameras. Needless to say he was always the villain. I remember John Le Mesurier used to tell, in that gentle, humorous voice of his, how he had once seen Den-Den being bundled into a police van outside the Intrepid Fox in Wardour Street. Not wishing to get involved he had merely said in passing, 'Ah, Dennis, working?'

He once came in brandishing a leg of lamb, demanding that I put it in the fridge. God knows where he had found it but either it was nicked or it really had fallen off the back of a lorry. His trick was to eat his meal, wash it down with a great deal of wine, then create a scene and storm out leaving the rest of the company to pay his share. He always wanted just to sign the bill but I would never let him – until one day I was so fed up with him I allowed him to do so . . . I knew I wouldn't see him again and I paid it with a great sense of relief. It was worth it; by then he was barred from every pub in Soho.

I wasn't too impressed by the rather raffish lot that used to come from Chelsea around about the time the Kings Road was becoming fashionable in the gossip columns – not because they were a bit boisterous and full of themselves, but because they always let one young woman pay the bill. She was very sweet and we often chatted while she waited for her guests, something I always tried to find time for if I saw a woman sitting alone. When, having noticed that nobody else ever attempted to put their hands in their pockets, I started to place the bill in the middle of the table, just to nudge their consciences. It didn't work. One day I told her she was far too kind. At the time I had no idea that she was Henrietta Guinness and could well afford to foot the bill; even when I found out, I thought they were a bit creepy to let her pay all the time – but I also realised that their standards were none of my business. I liked her enormously, and of course I thoroughly approved when she married an Italian fisherman and had a baby daughter. I thought that after the silly, hectic years of racing around with the takers and hangers-on she had found happiness.

Two of Henrietta Guinness's real friends were Wayne Sleep and his manager George Lawson. George was very fond of her and one evening when he was having dinner with his mother I asked him how she was; had he heard from her recently? He said he was a bit worried about her and thought it was time he went to visit her. I told him to give her my love and tell her I was longing to see the baby, which was then six months old. A few days later her suicide was reported in all the papers. She had thrown herself off a bridge, poor little soul. Dear George came in absolutely heartbroken; he was really sobbing and wished he had gone to see her. He had known something was wrong. I tried to comfort him and look after him but it would be just that evening that we ran out of the white wine he was drinking, Corvo Bianco. He followed me into the servery where we kept the fridge, and there he found a bottle of Orvieto Secco which came from the area in Italy where Henrietta lived and died. He broke down again and hugged the bottle as his last connection with her, poor darling. I know drink often releases emotions but they are still painful to see; and I wasn't feeling too strong myself.

I would have had to be blind, deaf and dumb not to have noticed how drink affects people – and sometimes the line between comedy and disaster can be very fine. Not being much of a drinker myself (just having the odd small brandy and water if I'm tired) I've been able to be objective over the years and sometimes somebody else's disaster had been my belly laugh – though tactfully, only when they've gone. Bill Grundy, the great journalist and television personality, was always reluctant to go home and would spend hours trying to persuade me to give him a bottle to take back with him. I would try and tell him he'd had enough but one night it was so late and I was so tired I gave in.

'Here you are Bill, now go home.'

He left as last but went and dropped the bottle on the stairs. He was so upset you would have thought it was a major tragedy but I'm afraid that as soon as I had shut the door on him I burst out laughing. My laughter wasn't really unkind – but it can be a hell of a relief to catch the last bus home.

Bill was mostly well loved by his colleagues but he was quite well known for getting himself into trouble and there was one memorable day when he must have said something untoward. He and Isobel Daly were at a table with another couple. I had served him soup and the others were having salad. The place was packed and I was very busy when there was a disturbance at Bill's table. When I looked round one of the young ladies was just emptying a plate of salad over Bill's head, which was very low over the soup, after which she marched out. I rushed to see if he was all right and offered to clean up the splashed soup. 'Never mind about the soup, what about my fucking head,' he demanded. Fortunately he was quite uninjured but I had to spend a lot of time picking the bits of salad out of his hair.

Yet Bill could behave impeccably when he was having dinner with the likes of Sir Neville Cardus, a charming man whom he admired tremendously. They would talk about cricket and music together for hours. Sadly the time came when, Bill said, Sir Neville was too frail to make the stairs any more. Bill wrote the most beautiful obituary in the *Spectator* when Sir Neville died in 1975. It was about an evening when Sir Neville had decided that after a lifetime of listening to all kinds of composers he had decided that Mozart was the greatest. The evening I remember best is one when to the astonishment of myself and the customers he suddenly stood up and sang 'Dove Sono', the Countess's song from *The Marriage of Figaro*, in a light but tuneful voice; there was delighted applause from all of us when he had finished. Bill may have been a lovable pest at times but that night he contributed to a very happy evening.

The menu at Bianchi's was comfortable but varied which didn't stop a lot of people coming in for just their favourite meal. James Orr loved Scampi Newburg and would send letters from all over the country or abroad booking a table well ahead and adding a tentative query at to whether we could manage to have this particular dish on the menu that day. Somehow the chef always did. Beryl Reid preferred chicken livers *trifolati*, that is cooked in marsala on rice. She had been coming to Bianchi's since her mother first brought her when she was eleven. She used to say cheerfully she hated me – I was older than her, yet I had more energy – though she was no slouch and I never heard of her missing a performance. She was wicked one day when she overheard a customer on his way out telling me how much he had enjoyed himself, how wonderful he thought the food and the service were. She looked at him: 'More than I can say for mine – dreadful!' He looked appalled, and perhaps both of our faces were a picture because she burst out laughing and agreed with him: of course it was wonderful.

Another joker was Bryan Izzard, the television director. A whole crowd of people came up the stairs one night and I was a bit flustered because the room was almost full and they hadn't booked. Suddenly, booming behind them, was Bryan, a great big bear of a man and a very dear regular.

'So, you're not going to give us a table, are you? Well, we'll go elsewhere, come along.' And he gathered everyone up and stormed down the stairs.

I was flabbergasted. Bryan was such a friend and I hadn't had a chance to explain. Ten minutes later he was back with just two friends, the wretch, grinning all over his face.

'Sorry about that, Elena, but I just didn't want to entertain that lot.'

I was so relieved, but what a performance!

The total reverse of impatient was Paul Schofield, who was quite happy to stand and chat while waiting for a table. He had his haircut somewhere nearby and was always alone – except for one occasion when he lunched with a lady. They were obviously old friends, and after lunch she took out a little bag and emptied some very pretty beach-stones in front of him. I couldn't help admiring them and she told me she collected them as a hobby and polished them to bring out their beauty. She had brought a selection for Paul Schofield to choose from and I thought it was such a sweet idea – so very apt for such a natural gentleman.

Another actor I was very fond of was Peter Bull, a dear, open-hearted man who told me his worries and wrote to me when he was lonely on tour abroad. It sometimes amazes me that people forget that actors are very vulnerable: they are often out of work for long periods and they, too, have financial crises; but people seem to think if they have a famous face they don't have any problems. Luckily for them their own profession does understand which is why they like their own company so much. Peter Bull was a great friend of Albert Finney, and that bond of affection still binds together those of us who loved him. Peter never forgot my birthday and I still have all the Bully Bear books he gave me.

Albert Finney sometimes says to me, 'Elena, do you remember when we were poor?' and I laugh and tell him, 'A bookmaker's son is never poor.' He is a lovely customer who followed me to L'Escargot. One evening he booked a table for six at ten thirty, after a show, but as his guests arrived they announced they would be fourteen. I rang down to the chef who was just about ready to pack up and told him I didn't mind what he sent up but fourteen meals I must have, I'd sort them out at the table. I told everyone it was no use looking at the menu, they would have to accept whatever arrived. There was I shouting, 'Who wants chicken? Who wants lamb?' and somehow it all worked out. When I told Albert this would have to be the arrangement, he said, 'Quite right Elena. If we were at home with Mother we would have to eat what she gave us.' So it was all very jolly and they enjoyed themselves – which is how I like an evening to end.

A friend of Peter and Albert's was a young actor called Kerwin Matthews who played Johann Strauss in *The Great Waltz*. He was a sweet young man, and when he was sent on location to Vienna he let Peter know that he was homesick for Bianchi's. So I sent him a box of *amaretti*, the biscuits which are served with *zabaglione*, and he was thrilled that anybody should care for him all those miles away. He hates flying so I don't see much of him now but he writes every Christmas from California and we exchange family news. He has given up acting for antiques and landscape gardening.

Talking of *zabaglione*, it was such a favourite with some customers that they sometimes escaped from dinner parties in other restaurants just for that one treat. I never minded, I understood. The one who actually took the biscuit, so to speak, was Lionel Stander, the actor with the great gravelly voice. He once ate three at one sitting; I couldn't believe it when he called for the third one – but it went down with as much enjoyment as the first.

When Philip Saville brought Louis Jourdan in for lunch one day the waitresses went all of a flutter and you couldn't blame them – he was so incredibly handsome. At the end of their meal I told him how much I had enjoyed his performance in *Gigi*.

'Ah, but you will not like the next role that Philip has directed me in; I play somebody horrible,' he replied in the delicious accent.

'That's all right. I don't get to see television because I'm working so I can always remember you from the film.'

I meant it and still do.

Not everyone had Louis Jourdan's charm and Charles Laughton frightened the life out Pierina, one of the waitresses, with his, 'I'll have a sherry. Now leave us, child.' Poor Pierina was too scared to go back with the sherry so I had to take it. I knew what she meant; he had an overwhelming and rather unpleasant presence. Another waitress, Mary, was scared of dear Frank Norman because he had a curved scar on one side of his face which he had acquired in his early days as a bum in Soho – although by now he was the highly respected author of *Fings Ain't What They Used To Be*. He was always immaculately dressed and a lavish host; it gave him pleasure to be generous after his deprived childhood. His scar certainly didn't prevent him from having a string of good-looking upper-class girlfriends.

Another customer who caused a stir was David McCallum; now to me he was just that nice-looking boy who had been coming in with his parents since the fifties. I had no idea that he was the star of a television series called *The Man from UNCLE*. I'm afraid that if they weren't on on Sunday evenings I didn't recognise them, but the advertising girls in the restaurant knew who he was and got very excited. Funny how fame affects people.

I don't know if it was quite fame that affected the actress Marieka Riviera who used to come in with Laurence Harvey. She was very exotic with a magnificent bosom which she did little to hide. Nevertheless she resented people looking at her. One evening she got particularly huffy and as she left said to Aldo, who was in charge of the cash desk in those days, 'I don't mind you looking at my titties, Aldo, but I don't want anyone else looking.' Poor Aldo, he didn't know where to put himself.

It was probably Laurence Harvey who recommended Bianchi's to Simone Signoret. She came regularly with her English agent and was a very womanly woman, gentle and gracious, always taking the time to ask about my children. She was beautiful and certainly didn't eat a lot them, so why she became so overweight later I could never understand.

It wasn't all actors, of course; there were designers like Hardy Amies and Clive who used to invite me to their collections because they knew I had been trained in their profession. I loved going to the shows, though I felt rather nervous among those grand fashion ladies from the magazines and newspapers.

There were masses of journalists from both ends of the spectrum. Apart from the political writers who hung out with MPs there were the crime reporters lunching with senior police officers – and a whole bunch from the *Daily Mirror* who seemed never to have to go back to the office. In fact the only way to get rid of them was to direct them to the many afternoon drinking clubs around Soho.

Most of these places had started out as clubs for the catering industry, somewhere for waiters and chefs to go between closing up after lunch and opening for dinner. They were men's clubs mostly, few women would have gone except, perhaps, the occasional accompanied actress. A lot of them were Italian-owned and the men played cards, darts and had a drink. A typical one was Cavalli's, above the Café Bleu, but the Caterers' Club in Frith Street was where Jimmy Edwards, Tommy Cooper, Stanley Baxter and Albert Dimes played darts and cards. Then there was the Campari Club at the top of Frith Street, which had a mixture of catering people, businessmen and journalists, and Sorrento's, run by Nina, which had a little dance-floor so women were welcome there though not, as far as I remember, the ladies of the street. They were friendly, well-run places, not at all like the sleazy rip-off joints of today, but you had to be known to the management. A recommendation from Bianchi's was sufficient but we were expected to be careful not to send the sort who could get aggressively drunk.

Tempers could flare unexpectedly among normally well-behaved people and I've witnessed a scene or two that would have you believing the persons involved would never speak to each other again. But these things are inclined to be soon forgotten or overlooked in Soho, where paths are going to cross all the time. Sometimes I didn't even know the customers involved. They would appear to the quite happy then all hell would break loose. I remember a party of six at a certain table one evening. I was just walking away when out of the corner of my eye I saw this girl raise her arm and smash a glass right over this poor bloke's head. She rushed out without a word and I had to clear it up without letting the other customers be disturbed, quite tricky really. The only thing to do when something like that happens is bring the bill as quickly as possible and ask them all to leave. But one girl I did have sympathy with on another occasion was at the large table with John Taylor, who was then the editor of *Tailor and Cutter* and wrote witty columns in *Weekend* and other papers. I overheard him saying (you couldn't help it, the pitch was so high), 'You're only a bookmaker's daughter,' in a manner so nasty that I turned round just in time to see her throw her coffee at him before she, too, marched out.

John Taylor was a regular, eating there almost everyday, so when he rang the following morning to see if he could come back I told him: 'Now I've washed the bloody wall down, yes.' He had, perhaps appropriately, a very cutting tongue and could be very amusing, but there was one day when he didn't amuse me at all. Michael Ivens, an industrial journalist and dear friend, was sitting with his girlfriend Kate (she is now his wife) when John Taylor asked me to take a note to their table, which I did. But when I saw Michael's reaction my instinct told me something was wrong. He just folded it up and put it in his inside pocket. I thought it might be something to upset Kate, who was obviously in love with him, so I insisted on seeing it. The note said, 'Do you know that Elena is in love with you?' I was furious but John Taylor just laughed, not realising that he could have made serious mischief. Supposing Michael had believed it; he may have been too embarrassed to come to the restaurant again and I would never have known why.

Still I must have forgiven him for when I had a telephone call from his great friend Jack Elvin who was trying to get in touch with him to tell him that Mrs Taylor had been in a car accident, I sent a member of staff round to Gaston's to find him and left messages everywhere. He came in in the evening with a girlfriend, rang home and rushed off. I'm afraid the girl was not all that sympathetic – just livid.

A funny thing is that in all the years I knew him John Taylor never once invited me to call him by his first name, yet Sir Timothy Bligh, who was just plain Mister when we first met, insisted on being called Tim. When he was knighted I asked him what he wanted me to call him now. 'Just keep on calling me Tim,' was his reply. Bill Heseltine, too, who was also knighted later, is still just Bill.

Sadly, Mr Taylor and I fell out over a piece of steak. He had just got off the train from Birmingham and it must have been at the end of a hard day as when he arrived at Bianchi's he was not in a good humour. I thought he was tired and suggested a spaghetti but he chose a steak instead. It was early evening so there were none of his friends about, not even his girlfriend, and solitude did nothing to improve his mood. When the steak arrived that was not to his liking either. I offered to take it back but nothing would pacify him and he stormed out, swearing that he would never enter the premises again. It was a promise which he kept, despite the efforts of his brother Bill and his friends Jack Elvin and David Hill to persuade him not to be so stubborn. But he must have felt the loss because his friends continued to use the place where he had spent so many enjoyable afternoons – as I know only too well – while I watched the clock and wondered when I would get my break. What a silly way to end thirty years of friendship.

Seven

Over the years there have been many comical scenes. Mr Cornish, a travel agent, used to bring in groups of Russian diplomats who always arrived with their own vodka, and goodness, could they eat and drink! At the end of each meal they would cover me with Russian medals. I don't know what they were for but I had to wear them until they left, and that usually took a long time. One day they wanted me to go back to the embassy with them, there was a party going on. No, I said, I had to go home to see my children. They persuaded Piero, the manager of downstairs Bianchi's, to go with them; when he came back for the evening shift he said the party was still going on. I said I knew it was as they kept ringing to say the party was not complete without me; they even sent an embassy car to fetch me but I'm afraid they had to take *niet* for an answer.

I don't suppose it was that afternoon that gave Piero the taste for the high life, but he certainly got himself into plenty of trouble. It's not difficult to know other people's business around Soho so I knew he was gambling heavily. Then one evening, very late when I was clearing up, he came up the stairs extremely agitated, scared stiff in fact. He told me there were two men downstairs who wanted to see the owner who by that time was Mr Petti; he didn't have to tell me why. So I went down and there indeed were two enormous chaps.

I told them that Piero was only the working partner and that Mr Petti was in Italy. All this time their eyes were roving round the place and I could see what was on their minds. They were going to do enough damage to frighten someone into paying up.

'Do you know Albert Dimes?' I said.

'Yes, why?'

'He's a great friend of mine and he eats here. I don't think he'd be too happy if you did any damage to this place.'

They looked hard at me and gave a reluctant look round but they left without another word.

You'd think an occurrence like that would have taught Piero a lesson; well, I suppose it did and it didn't. Over the weekend he did a bunk, but not before he had gone all round the manor borrowing money. His con was that all the customers had paid by cheque and that as Mr Petti was in Italy he had no cash for the staff wages. He got money out of Pete King of Ronnie Scott's, the Villa Cesare and several other restaurants. What none of them knew is that I always had the wages made up in cash and had already paid the staff.

Piero surfaced later in the Bahamas and I believe is now somewhere in Florida. News of him travels back to Soho now and again from every corner of the world. He won't come back which is probably sad for him because everyone misses the place when they are away for long; it wouldn't be the money that people remembered but the fact that he ran off and left his wife and children destitute.

On the subject of comical scenes, there is always one person who doesn't find it funny at the time. Bryan Izzard, a television producer for Thames TV, and his secretary were having dinner in the big room when I heard a kind of strangled scream from their table. The girl was as white as a sheet and just managed to gulp out, 'Something's just run up my leg.' I guessed at once what it was. A mouse. I ran to the cash desk where Aldo was working and whispered what had happened. We pulled the table back and there you could see the shape of the thing under her trouser suit – and it was getting very close to her lap up her flared trousers. Aldo gave the poor girl's thigh an almighty whack and the mouse ran back down her leg like the one in the nursery rhyme, *Hickery, Dickery, Dock*. It got a final wallop, then Aldo swept it up and popped it in a dustbin. I had to explain that it was the fault of Kiki the restaurant cat who, although she was an excellent mouser, would insist upon bringing her victims *into* the place.

Thank heavens it hadn't happened to one of Bryan's regular guests, Hilda Baker, who was always in a bit of doo-dah when she was working. Bryan would ring me and say she was in something of a state and would I find a cosy table and look after her especially well? She was a star, after all, so I made sure that she felt that nothing was too much trouble. I was glad I had been able to be indulgent when we all found out later that her nervous state had been due to Alzheimer's Disease.

And I won't forget the occasion when Tania Heyworth and John Wolfers, both from publishing, were sitting at table 5 by the window one summer evening. I don't know what prompted it but suddenly Tania threw all her rings out of the window. I was shocked thinking they might be valuable and I ran down the stairs to look for them in the gutter. Freddy the barrow boy who kept a fruit stall outside Bianchi's asked what I was looking for and when I told him fished the rings out of his pocket. They had landed on his stall. I took them back upstairs to return them to Tania but she waved them away saying that she never wanted to see them again. By now I could see they were dress rings, of nothing except perhaps sentimental value, so I put them in my bag for safe-keeping. A year or so later I reminded her of the incident and she had completely forgotten that I had rescued them. However, she *did* seem pleased to see them again.

One evening I was in the servery when this panic-stricken girl rushed in to say her boss, Mr Raynor, whom I knew well, had fainted into his grapefruit. When I asked her what she had done to him she looked blankly at me and, sure enough, when I got to his table the silly bitch had left him face-down in the grapefruit. I lifted his head and wiped his face and he went on with what he had been saying as if nothing had happened, telling me that he was off to a concert at the Festival Hall. I was worried but, like the old joke, there was a doctor in the restaurant who promised to keep an eye on him should it happen again – which it did. I rang his wife to alert her to meet him at the station and she kindly called me back to say he was OK and the doctor could find nothing wrong. It was all very odd but quite comical when I knew he was all right.

Being concerned about customers has always been part of my life but I'll never forget Lady Parker, the American wife of the Lord Chief Justice. They had been having dinner and, as we usually shut the downstairs door soon after eleven, I escorted her out while His Lordship settled the bill. We were standing in the street chatting when she spotted the two men in a doorway further up the street towards Soho Square.

'What goes on in there?' she wanted to know.

'Oh, it's just one of those near-beer places.' I didn't

want her to know it was a very disreputable Maltese club for pimps, girls and touts. Now she was a very formidable-looking lady, impeccably groomed with white-rimmed dark glasses, and she was striding up that street before I could stop her – and halfway up the passage that led to the club before I could catch up with her. I think the men on the door were so astonished that they were rooted to the spot.

'Lady Parker, Lady Parker,' I called 'Lord Parker, your husband, is waiting for you.' I knew that would stop anyone even thinking of getting heavy, and to my relief she turned and came back. Being concerned as a hostess-cum-manageress was one thing, but being responsible for the safety of the wife of the Lord Chief Justice was slightly more than I needed at the end of a long day.

'I just wanted to see,' she said mildly.

Responsibility and honesty must go together but sometimes they can make resentful bedfellows. The night Tim Behrens, the painter, and Patricia Chaplin, who had been married to Charlie Chaplin's son, left a plastic bag in the restaurant has to be an example of that. The bag was full of cash – lots and lots and lots of notes. Well, of course, I expected Tim Behrens to rush in the next day worrying about it. I thought he had probably sold a picture for cash and I stashed it away safely in the back of my locker. But nobody rang or called by and I didn't know how to get hold of Tim. I couldn't tell anyone about it as there were enough rogues among his friends who would say they had been told to collect it. Weeks later the girlfriend (or whatever) turned up and again I confided that they had left a bag: 'Oh, is that where I left it,' she replied. No sigh of relief, just a casual acceptance when I handed it over.

She didn't even check the contents, let alone say thank you and offer a small reward. It probably never occurred to her that for me that bag contained the equivalent of many, many months' wages. I think the bus journey home that day was a little harder than most; not that I was discontented with my lot, but when you meet people to whom money means nothing a little despair can set in.

People lose lots of things in restaurants, often from being distracted because they have stayed longer than they should. They rush off leaving hats, umbrellas or macs. These are easy to deal with; you simply put them on one side with a label. Other things can cause real anxiety all round. I remember Peter Finch getting into a terrible state when he was having lunch with Kay Kendall; he had lost his good-luck charm, a rabbit's paw, and thought he must have dropped it in a taxi. He turned out every pocket but there was no sign of it. He had to leave to go the rehearsals and I could see he was sincerely distressed. I found it later under the table and managed to track him down through friends and get it back to him.

Another time that had me on my hands and knees was when Faye Dunaway came in because her husband-to-be, the photographer Terry O'Neill, had lost his watch. They had had dinner earlier and Terry had noticed the loss when they were in Ronnie Scott's just across the road. It must have been an amazing sight to see that beautiful filmstar and myself scrabbling under the table. We couldn't find it and she was most upset because she knew it was precious to him; it had belonged to his late father. I knew he had been wearing it in the restaurant as he had shown it to me. We went across to Ronnie's to tell him it wasn't at Bianchi's and, of course, it was dark in Ronnie's so there was no chance of finding it there. Then I had a flash of inspiration. I had noticed that the watch strap was too big for him and suggested he looked up his sleeve. And there it was, it had rolled up his arm. It was only later that it occurred to me that he had the most monumental cheek sending one of the world's most celebrated actresses to do his errands; but I knew him well and shouldn't have expected anything different.

I still think the funniest enquiry for something lost I ever received was from a Mr Bruce, a gentleman who even in 1966 wore spats and carried a walking stick. He had once asked me if I had ever been to the ballet and on hearing that I hadn't wrote me a formal letter inviting me to the Royal Opera House to see *Swan Lake* with dinner at Chez Solange beforehand. Well, there was no way I could get an evening off to go to the ballet with a customer, even if I had wanted to. I wasn't too sure of his motives, either, so I declined his invitation. He still came in for dinner on his own and was always polite, but when he rang one morning to ask if he had left his false teeth in the restaurant it was all I could do not to laugh out loud. It puzzled me all day and still does: how on earth can you lose your false teeth?

One of the most frequent mistakes made during the winter months at a small restaurant is the taking of the wrong overcoat, understandable as one navy coat looks pretty much like another, particularly when a few too many have been taken as well. As a rule it can be dealt with quite amicably: the person who has 'inherited' the expensive number is usually the first to return it. Not always though. John Broderick the novelist had dinner with his publisher Marion Boyars and her husband one evening, and although I hadn't seen him go he had had to be helped out of the place and into a taxi, not unusual for quite a few of my customers. He must have pointed at the wrong coat which his friends helped him on with. But what a commotion when the real owner, a Mr Raki from the Middle East, discovered the mistake. He was screaming and demanding we call the police. I was trying to pacify him, telling him it wasn't a theft and all the time trying to track down the hotel John was staying in. Eventually we found it and I sent the cloakroom girl to make the exchange. It was obvious that Mr Raki felt he had fallen into a den of thieves because he insisted that his chauffeur drive the girl there. When they arrived John was fast asleep on the bed still wearing the coat which they gently removed, leaving his own. John came into lunch the next day and never said a word; I don't think he had any idea of what had happened.

I never saw Mr Raki again but John was a frequent and welcome visitor. One day he invited me to a friend's house for lunch. It was a lovely party and afterwards he took me into the garden and handed me a copy of his latest book. 'Here you are Elena, this is for you.' I was very pleased and asked him to sign it for me which he did. Then he turned to another page and showed it to me: he had dedicated the book to me with the beautiful words: 'For Elena Salvoni, who has done more for the arts in London than will ever be known. A small tribute to her wisdom, sympathy and glorious sense of life.' I was completely, utterly stunned and will treasure that moment all my life.

Eight

Soho in the fifties was the kind of place that attracted people who felt at home in its rather raffish atmosphere; it wasn't as fashionable as it is now, but what a variety of customers we had, many of them hard-up and yet to become famous. I remember Bruce and Jeffrey Bernard from the Café Bleu days, the same good-looking boys, scraping a living from building sites, a bit of backstage work and whoever would pay for the meal of the day. Because Soho belongs to today, every today, I was fascinated to be reminded by Daniel Farson's book *Soho in the Fifties* of many old names and faces. The Roberts Colquhoun and MacBryde, Dylan Thomas and Brendan Behan, as well as David Archer, George Melly and Francis Bacon who often lunched together. I didn't know what they did, only that they all seemed to have a lot of friends. George and Francis are still friends though as I said before Francis did sniff a bit when he first came into the refurbished L'Escargot: 'It looks like an ice-cream parlour, Elena.' But since he likes the food he forgives us.

The appearance of the Establishment Club in Greek Street in the early sixties changed a lot of attitudes towards Soho; the kind of people who wouldn't be seen dead outside Mayfair started to discover it and the resurgence of vitality was reflected in people's dress and manners. I began to hear language that I had been brought up to believe only belonged to the gutter in the mouths of street gangs being bandied about among friends. It didn't faze me at all but I had to consider regulars like Father Ferguson, who came up from the country for the occasional treat. (We used to give him a set meal of a bowl of soup, half a serving of risotto and a coffee for five shillings and sixpence.)

The Italian–Catholic–Soho connection has always been strong. When Father Bill Kirkpatrick started Centrepoint, a refuge for the young homeless in St Anne's crypt, I used to take all the leftover bread round each night on my way to catch the last bus. And Father Camillo from St Peter's Italian Church in Clerkenwell once helped me get the younger brother of one of the waitresses out of prison. He was the chauffeur of a millionaire who turned out to be a very clever crook that the police had been trying to catch for over two years. Luckily he knew nothing about his boss's business and Father Camillo was able to get him legal representation and an early release. Sadly, this is very much part of his job these days and his desk is always piled high with letters from youngsters in prison; he replies to them all and visits as many as he can, at the same time writing reassuring letters (not always confiding the whole truth) to their families in Italy. A lovely and true priest, he still sometimes comes to L'Escargot. I've had the odd letter from customers inside myself; one particular friend, a charming and generous man, wrote to me when he was in for embezzlement and still writes every Christmas. Quite a few have spent the odd night in either Bow Street or Vine Street.

When the phone rang late one night announcing a call from Vine Street my first reaction was to put my hand over the receiver to tell the staff to take the glasses off the tables – it was one thirty and our licence only ran until midnight. Then they said they had a customer of mine in custody and the only way to get him to quieten down was to promise to let me know where he was. I told them he was a really nice chap, just a bit boisterous in booze, and they told me they would let him out on bail in an hour or two if he had settled down. I rang his girlfriend who had obviously had enough of his behaviour because she bellowed out, 'I'm not bloody going,' and slammed the phone down. I felt sorry for him, but there was nothing I could do about it.

The influence of the Establishment Club crowd was fun and brought in a new group of people who were also to become lifelong friends, among them Johnny Dankworth and Cleo Laine. He didn't drink anything and I was never quite sure if it was because he couldn't afford to; musicians weren't paid much then. One lunchtime they started making music with spoons and forks, glasses and coffee cups. Mr Bianchi wanted to stop them but I told him to leave them alone; they were only young and having fun.

Ned Sherrin used to come in with Caryl Brahms and years later when I was visiting Aldo's sister, Anselma, in New York, a production of his was on Broadway – *Side By Side With Sondheim*. After I'd seen the show one evening he took me to Charlie's, a fashionable bar on 45th Street. It was absolutely packed; there were two heavy gentlemen at the door and I thought I had walked into an old gangster film. There was a great long bar and being short I really couldn't see anything much. Suddenly a voice shouted, 'Elena, have you come over to open a restaurant?' It was a dear regular, a lady teacher who came over to England every summer to catch up on the London theatre. Everyone turned to look at me and Ned said with mock indignation, 'And I thought *I* was famous.'

Parts of New York and Soho are very much alike, in that people of the same interests seem to find similar places and want to be together. I have a connection of which I am very proud with the Odeon on Broadway and the Café Luxembourg on West 70th Street. They came about because Alan Bennett was in a play over there and a young actor in the cast, Keith McNally, was doing a bit of 'moonlighting' as a waiter. He decided that he preferred New York to London and the restaurant business to acting, so Alan asked me to write him a reference so he could get a permit. I did it willingly, he got his green card, worked hard and is now a very successful proprietor. How I love it when people succeed in what they really want to do.

Nine

Things were changing round Islington too. The house next door that had been burnt to the ground was rebuilt into four little flatlets, and the street was beginning to be quite smart but was still very friendly. As our new neighbours moved in we all introduced ourselves, which is how I met Joe Orton and Kenneth Halliwell.

They were an absolutely enchanting couple of boys, both very good-looking, and they seemed very happy just watching the kids play in the street. When they went away they would empty their fridge and give the contents to us; it was never very much, just an egg, a bit of butter or cheese – they were so hard up all the time, poor dears – and when they were due back I would always leave something for them to come home to. Sometimes they came round for a cup of tea on Sunday afternoon and on one occasion Aldo, who was a marvellous storyteller – he always had the children's complete attention – asked Joe how he learned to write. Joe replied very simply, 'Ken taught me; I tell him my ideas and he writes them down.' They obviously adored each other; they went everywhere together, and when Joe's mum died and he had to go to Leicester for the funeral, poor Ken was absolutely lost on his own.

They were very good friends to my son Louie and I can state with total honesty I never had a moment's uneasiness when he was with them – they were not the sort of people to molest children. He came into the kitchen one day saying, 'Those boys next door must read an awful lot of books. I've just seen some of them being loaded into a van.' I thought nothing of it until the next day when I read that they had been sent to jail for defacing library books. The neighbours were all tut-tutting but I'm afraid when I read the details I found it all rather funny, typical of them, but it was an opinion I kept to myself.

When they came out after three months I met them in the street; they were completely unabashed and as cheeky as ever.

'Elena darling, I've had the most wonderful time,' said Joe.

'Oh, they put you together, did they?' I asked, all innocence as ever.

'No dear, that's why I had such a wonderful time.'

I tried to be severe – 'Now you just behave yourselves. Our rates have gone up because of you!' – but we all went on our way laughing.

I wasn't in a very jokey mood the day I came home from work after lunch and found Louie and his best friend, my nephew Dino, moping about in the kitchen. I asked them what was the matter and they said they had been playing tennis in the backyard (no, we don't have a court, their net was a piece of rope dividing the garden in half) when one of the ladies from the next door flatlets claimed the tennis balls belonged to her dogs. Having been brought up not to be rude to their elders, the boys had handed them over.

'Well, who did they belong to?' I wanted to know.

'A friend of the doctor's across the road gave them to us,' said Louie. 'He was cleaning out his car and asked if we'd like them.'

Now I didn't often take up the cudgels on the boys' behalf but I thought this was most unfair, so I charged up the stairs, banged on her door and said very firmly, 'I want my son's balls back. If your dogs needs balls you can go to Woollies and buy them – and next time you lose your budgie don't expect the boys to roam round the streets looking for him.' Most indignant I was, but I got them and gave them back to the kids.

A few minutes later there was a ring on the doorbell and there was Joe, hanging on to the railings, collapsing with laughter. 'Elena, Elena, Ken and I heard you asking for your son's balls back. It was the funniest thing ever,' and he started to roar with laughter again.

'Sssh, the whole street'll overhear. Go away. No tea for you today, you rotter,' and I slammed the front door. I think it took a good two cups of tea before I began to see the funny side.

Aldo and I were so proud of Joe's successes. When they came to tea on Sundays they would show us the newspaper cuttings and we all seemed to share the pleasure. It was Louie who first noticed a change in Ken.

'There's something wrong. I don't think he's very well,' was all he said. Ken had always talked to him about school and now he didn't seem interested, was distracted all the time.

Joe was being invited out more and more on his own; he was a sought-after name and good company, but they were still fairly hard-up. Joe used to use our phone in the morning. 'I can't call Terrence Rattigan from a call-box, Elena!' – a reminder that even in the sixties it was still difficult to get a phone installed.

When *Loot* was nominated for the Evening Standard Award Joe bought himself a new suit and came round to show it off to me. It was ghastly, the sort of thing that George Melly wears with great success, but it wasn't right on Joe.

'You look like Max Miller,' I told him bluntly. 'The reception is at Quaglino's where there's a great curved staircase – they'll all see you coming.' He looked a bit crestfallen and when I saw his picture in the paper the next day he had taken my advice and was wearing a neat navy-blue blazer.

When they went off to Morocco for their holiday I kept an eye on their flat. I didn't need a key because they had a huge letter-box for all the scripts and books that arrived and I could just peer in through this to check. I found the card they sent me only the other day; so sad... they were so happy... And they were happy when they returned, looking smashing with their deep tans. They said they had really enjoyed themselves and had lots of snaps of people I know. 'But we've got to sort them out first,' said Joe with a mischievous grin; I could guess which ones I wouldn't be shown. As it happened I never got to see any of them.

Aldo bumped into Joe in the street the next evening and invited him to the pub where he had his daily bottle of Guinness, but Joe refused, saying he was off to Elstree to see Brian Epstein the following morning to discuss a £100,000 contract. We were all very excited and kept our fingers crossed for him.

At that time Aldo was in rather poor health so Louie would sit in with him while I went to work. Coming home at around two in the morning I glanced up at our bedroom window to see if Aldo was asleep which he obviously was as there were no lights on. But what did surprise me was that Joe and Ken's light was still on. They always went to bed early – a habit left over from the days when they tried to save on electricity – but I thought no more of it; I was tired.

The next day off I went to work, reminding Aldo that the boys were coming round with their holiday snaps in the afternoon. At eleven fifteen that morning a chauffeur arrived for Joe, went up to their door and knocked; nobody answered so he came to our house to check that he had the right address. My younger brother, Mario, who has a flat downstairs, saw that the chauffeur was upset – he was muttering about something strange going on next door – so he went with him, looked through the letter-box and saw Ken lying on the floor. Mario called the police who smashed the door down and found them both dead, Joe covered in blood and Ken dead of a massive overdose.

I knew nothing of this so when I came home for my afternoon break and saw the BBC and ITV television vans outside Joe's door I naïvely thought, marvellous, Joe's had a hit, and I came down the road smiling at his good fortune. There were lots of press outside and they were just about to question me when Aldo dragged me indoors.

'Joe must have had a hit,' I said happily.

'He's had a hit all right,' said Aldo, 'Ken's hit him with a hammer. He's dead, Elena, they are both dead.'

It was terrible, horrible. There was such a jumble of thoughts . . . the fact that it had taken place in the room next to our bedroom and neither Aldo nor Louie had heard a thing, that their last gesture had been to give Louie and Dino their bikes because they could now afford to travel by public transport. The boys had been out on the bikes that morning and it was when they were putting them back in the shed at the end of Joe's garden that they heard what had happened. On top of it all my daughter Adriana was expecting our first grandchild. The phone was by the window and I sat there waiting for my son-in-law to ring and trying not to look like a nosy-parker, but I couldn't help seeing the coffins brought out.

How I managed to go back to work that night I'll never know. Seeing the placards along the bus-route kept making it real, yet I couldn't accept it; hearing people discuss it in the restaurant as a shocking but gossipy event was hard, too, but I never said a word. So I was truly furious when the *Daily Mirror* ran a piece about them three days later saying they were always having screaming rows. They lived right next door to me and all I ever heard was the sound of the typewriter and one of them singing snatches of opera – happy sounds as far as I was concerned. It was a neighbour, Lily, who lived three doors away who had supplied them with the story; I could have wrung her neck. Years later a young couple came regularly to Bianchi's; he was in the advertising business, Barry Pritchard, and his wife was pregnant. It was before the days of cheque cards and when he first wrote his address on the back I saw that it was Joe's old flat. I told them we were neighbours and left it at that.

After some months Barry came to me and said, 'Why didn't you tell us, Elena?'

'Look you're a young married couple,' I told him, 'I didn't have the heart.'

He said that the news had so upset his wife that she couldn't bear to be in the flat alone and they would have to move. I asked him who had told them and, of course, it was Lily. I wished I had wrung her neck the first time.

Twenty years later Alan Bennett invited me to the

press preview of *Prick up Your Ears*, Joe's life story; Alan had written the screenplay. I came out absolutely shaken – Gary Oldman was so like Joe it was like being in his company all over again. I was less pleased with Alfred Molina's portrayal of Ken. Personally I thought he was wrongly cast. Ken was every bit as handsome as Joe, masculine too, not in the least bit camp, dozy or sinister. I know some people didn't like him, or at least they preferred to be seen with Joe, who was the star. There are lots of people like that even when the relationship is heterosexual. I suppose Ken was frightened – felt threatened – by Joe's meteoric success. I know he worried about it because one time when a house on the other side of the road was for sale I urged Joe to buy it. He was making enough money to consider a mortgage.

'But what if Joe dries up?' was Ken's anxious response.

'Keep the flat and rent it out; if you find you can't afford the house later on, you can always sell it for a profit,' was my advice. How I wish they had been able to take it.

Ten

The Honourable Michael Campbell was a very friendly customer who had a cottage in the country in the grounds of a stately home; he invited me and the family down one weekend when they were holding a steam fair on the estate and he asked us to pick up his housekeeper on the way. He forgot to mention that she was chronically car-sick. The journey was a small nightmare of stops and starts. Eventually we arrived at the great iron gates where we left the housekeeper to recover in the fresh air and drove on through the grounds to find not one cottage but six. We had no idea which one was Michael's. I got out and knocked at one and as the door was open stepped straight into a kitchen. There making lunch was George Baker, another customer. I don't know which of us was the more surprised. Michael himself lived two doors up and soon made us welcome.

It was a lovely party with John Hurt and Marie-Lise, an American whom I called Chickin-Lickin, because his party piece was to read or recite the story in a very suggestive fashion, and George and his family. Michael and John played croquet on the lawn with Louie who, although he was only just eighteen, was not in the least overawed by the fact that they were all famous; some of his parents' good sense about it being who you were rather than what you did had rubbed off, and I was very proud of him.

Several years later he told me when I came home that he had seen the most wonderful play on television with a man called John Hurt in the lead, and I reminded him that they had played croquet together. Later that year when I visited my sister-in-law in America she was going on about the same wonderful play, and told me the character in it was just like a man we used to see each Sunday in Clerkenwell after church. We would be hanging around chatting and this man with pink hair and a trailing pink scarf would saunter past, and we'd giggle like hell when he had gone round the corner. So when Quentin Crisp launched the paperback edition of *The Naked Civil Servant* at Bianchi's I asked him if he knew St Peter's Italian Church. Yes, he said, he had lived in Percy Circus. Somehow, what with John playing him, it all seemed another example of the Italian–Soho connection.

The sixties brought changed attitudes all round; towards homosexuals, towards standards of dress and towards infidelity. I began to see affairs blossoming and breaking up in no time at all, and although I couldn't approve of the men who took their wives and their mistresses to the same restaurant I realised it was none of my business. But one day it became very much so. A regular was dining with a lady who was neither his wife nor his mistress but the wife of one of his friends: it could have been totally innocent but my instinct told me it wasn't so I tucked them in a discreet corner. Just as well, for a few moments later her husband came in with another woman (who was really ugly, so I guessed there was nothing going on there) and I placed them in the corner of the main room. I knew trouble was brewing and I had to think fast. I told the first couple there was a call from America for the man, let's call him John, and while he was taking the supposed call I explained the situation. My instinct had been right; if it had been above-board the couples would have joined each other. As it was I had to devise an escape route. John went back to his table to tell the lady he had to return to the office straight away and I organised the waiters to line themselves round the second table and start shouting at each other in Italian – then I came storming in to demand what was going on. The customers were so intent on watching us (I was never known to raise my voice) that the guilty couple were able to slip out quite unnoticed behind our human screen. We fell about laughing in the servery after they had gone and the customers never did understand what had happened.

It may have been the mini-skirts or the advent of the Pill, but a lot of older men were keen to make fools of themselves over sexy young girls. Their own age group still didn't have a lot of money so they were quite happy to be escorted by older men who would foot the bill in their search for fun. One customer became so enamoured I used to think he'd gone ga-ga.

'She hasn't even cut her wisdom teeth,' I told him when he gushed about how much in love he was.

It made no difference. His wife, to whom he had been married for thirty years, found out and threw him out, and he set up home with the girl. Within weeks he was moaning to me about never having a clean shirt.

'Now you'll appreciate all your wife did for you,' was my only comment – and soon after that he went back to her.

That kind of behaviour always made me feel a bit uncomfortable and seeing the misery unfaithfulness caused I was all the happier to go home to my Aldo and the children. It just wasn't part of our sort of background where marriage vows really meant for better or for worse. We all stuck out the bad patches, as our parents had before us, and there have been very few divorces or separations in the Italian community.

Sometimes a love affair would develop into a second marriage but as a rule there is a lot of difference between genuine love and a bit of fun on the side. I often thought that if half the mischief-makers worked as hard as I did they wouldn't have so much energy to spare for emotional entanglement, but I kept such opinions to myself. I did help to prevent one unsuitable marriage taking place. One evening at Bianchi's I noticed a young man down on one knee, obviously proposing. I took one look at her face and could see that the idea wasn't at all welcome to her, so I tapped him on the shoulder.

'Get up off the floor, you're blocking the way and you'll trip one of the waiters. We've very busy tonight.'

He jumped up and apparently was so embarrassed he never mentioned the subject again that night. Many years later she asked me how I'd guessed.

'You should have seen your face,' I told her. It was as simple as that but she was eternally grateful.

Dennis Abey had cause to be eternally grateful, too. One lunchtime he joined a group of friends and they seemed to be having a jolly time when one of the party picked up Dennis's plate of spaghetti and emptied it over his head. Dennis's instant reaction was to snatch up the half-full carafe of wine and not to empty it over his friend's head but to hit him with it. I rushed across the room and grabbed it – how I don't know, as I am tiny and he is tall; maybe Quentin Joyce was right after all and I am the Mighty Atom, but it could have been a very ugly scene. Dennis was really shaken; he could have killed the man. The others all left hurriedly. I helped Dennis clean up and he paid the bill for the lot. If I hadn't got there in time he could have been paying a much higher price for years.

As it was he and Derek Banham (Mike Luckwell joined them later) set up the Moving Picture Company in Bianchi's over lunch. At the end of the meal they called for the bill and the change was just sixpence which they dropped.

'That's all we can give you, Elena,' they said as I picked it up.

'Then I'll keep it for luck for you all,' I said. I sellotaped it to a piece of card and put the date on it.

They flourished as the business went from strength to strength. I always reminded them that they would be nowhere without my lucky sixpence and I would take it out to show them it was still in safe keeping. Sadly, somebody stole my wallet one day and with it the sixpence which I treasured so much. The company was doing all right so I didn't worry too much. Then I noticed that I hadn't seen Dennis around lately so I asked among his friends, expecting they would say he was in New York or Los Angeles. They told me he had pulled out of the company and it turned out to have been on the very day I had had my wallet stolen. Later Mike Luckwell booked the whole of downstairs at L'Escargot for a party but he would tell me nothing except that I would read all about it in the papers next day. It seemed he had sold the Moving Picture Company for twenty-five million pounds. I could only hope the person who stole my wallet didn't inherit similar good fortune.

Eleven

Celebrations are very much part of Soho life. Sir Charles Groves the conductor celebrated his knighthood at Bianchi's. Indeed, quite a few people came straight from the Palace, all dressed up in their morning clothes, just to show me their medals; they knew I would be thrilled for them.

One of the greatest parties ever was the wedding of Andy and Janice Rork. They decided to get married on a Friday the thirteenth and booked the whole restaurant for the evening. Their friends had strung a banner right across Frith Street and they arrived on a number 13 bus with the best man dressed as the conductor waving a bottle of champagne. It was a marvellous evening with lots of people from the film and advertising industries. When it was time for the bride and groom to leave, the best man asked me for a champagne bucket and two glasses, which I provided, and we all trooped out to see them off. There was a limousine outside which I thought was for them, also an ambulance which I thought was odd. Their friends frog-marched them to the ambulance, opened the back doors and inside they had arranged a bed behind curtains and had put the champagne on a little table beside it. What a send-off.

Another mad party involving Andy was the evening after Poland had beaten England at football and they all trooped in to drown their sorrows. Dennis Abey was carrying an enormous Union Jack which I had to stash in the corner before it knocked all the customers' glasses off the tables. They insisted on eggs, bacon and fried bread, which I went to organise. When I came back into the room there was Andy standing on the table with his trousers round his ankles. All I said was, 'Get down, your food is ready.' Luckily most of the customers knew Andy so they weren't offended, and the evening became very jolly.

There were various groups you could rely on to get a bit boisterous and noisy. Tariq Ali and his friends from the London School of Economics were not very popular when they got over-excited about politics; indeed, several customers suggested I might consider dropping something unpleasant in his soup. Of course I didn't, but his crowd were very arrogant and could spoil the atmosphere. However, that was twenty years ago, when they were the centre of so much publicity – they are probably all very charming now.

Bad behaviour overnight was invariably followed by an apology the next day. A group from the advertising world, who nearly created a riot with the soda syphons one evening, presented no exception to this pattern. They had been on tequila, which was suddenly *the* fashionable drink among the young and those still hoping to pass as young. They all got far too exuberant for my liking and were about to turn on the customers as well as each other, so I had to separate them all and make them behave. They were big lads and the sight of me standing among them sorting them out must have been rather funny. With the apologetic bunch of flowers came a pair of boxing gloves. I hung them on the wall as a sort of humorous warning and still have them at home.

At that time Bianchi's was used by a lot of the boxing fraternity. Chris and Angelo Dundee, who were promoters, brought in people like Joey Giardello, Jack Kid Berg, Willie Pep, Carmen Basillio and Willie Pastrano who were all, or had been, world champions in their weight. Rocky Marciano came whenever he was in Britain and Henry Cooper was a regular until he fell in love with Albina, whose uncle owned Peter and Mario's in Gerrard Street. Then I lost him as a customer but not before he, like all the others, had signed my boxing gloves. Very precious they are, too.

Will Thorpe's table could also be relied upon to get a bit lively, but I was terribly shocked the night he came in with a large group of friends announcing that the following day he was going into hospital for major heart surgery; they all patted him on the back, said good luck and left him to pay the bill. Nobody thought to offer him a lift home or even considered that he might be scared at the prospect of dying. While he was in hospital I sent him a hamper of nice food and received a beautifully handwritten thank-you note saying that he would soon be well enough to come and torment me and Aldo again. Sure enough at one-thirty one night, when I was just packing up, I heard a voice from the street shouting 'Elena'. I went to the window and there was Will hollering, 'I'm alive, Elena, I'm alive.' It was obvious he had been putting his new heart to the test. I managed to persuade him to go home, but I was delighted to see him fit and well again.

I never mind seeing people get cheerful in their cups, but when some couples come through the door your heart sinks; you know damn well they'll be having a flaming row before they are half-way into the first course; then it's a matter of hovering to see they don't come to blows. There was one girl who came in with her married boyfriend. She was wearing a skimpy white dress to show off her magnificent tan but he was quite pale so they obviously hadn't been on holiday together. Before long she rushed into the servery covered in red wine; she said she had split it but I could tell from her face that it wasn't an accident. She went to the lavatory, and took the dress off and handed it to me through the crack in the door while her, by then abject, lover raced back to her flat to find another frock. Meanwhile, I tried to rinse the wine out and hung it up to dry in the servery. Mr Bianchi came and asked what on earth I was doing hanging out cloths – he thought it was a table napkin and I swear it wasn't much bigger.

Sometimes people get abusive in drink and sometimes just plain silly. Selena Scott reminded me of an evening she was there when somebody at the long table threw a melon at someone the other end. Naturally the man ducked and there was a shattering of glass as it went through the window. I scolded them and told them to behave themselves, then ran down the stairs to see if anyone had been hurt; a melon is quite heavy and if it had hit a passerby on the head it could have knocked him or her out. There was no sign of it in the street and, thankfully, nobody lying flat out on the pavement so I went back to clear up the mess and found the melon had bounced back and got caught in the curtains. It was naughty of them and they paid for the window but when I knew nobody had been hurt I found it funny too.

Mostly I could deal with the ones who got abusive in drink and would tell the staff to stay away from this or that table. There was one man whom I used to call Mr 'Strega', because he wanted so many of them at the end of his meal – and trying to tell a drunk that he's had enough is one of the most difficult tasks in the world. I could cope with him on my own as he was always alone and would eventually stumble off into the night without paying his bill. I would have to pay to make the till balance, but he would come in within a day or two, sober, and make amends having already sent either a letter or a telegram. This went on for quite some time and it was OK by me because, apart from the *stregas*, his bill was never very much, just a plate of spaghetti or so. However one day he came in with a young man who promptly ordered a very expensive three-course meal, including a steak. They were both very drunk so I asked them who was going to pay for the meal as I guessed that once again Mr Strega had left any ready cash he had in other people's tills. The young man got very excited and shouted at me that his grandfather was a Scottish millionaire.

'I don't care if he is a Scottish billionaire,' I told him calmly, 'why don't you ring him and ask if he will pay the bill. If not I'd like to see the cash first.'

He looked through his pockets and had exactly sixpence on him.

I turned to Mr Strega and said, 'I've stood for you and your behaviour for many years but I don't know this person from Adam and I'm damned if I am going to pay for him.'

The scene looked like getting quite nasty until a very large gentleman intervened saying, 'Nobody talks to Elena like that,' and they left.

I shut the front door on them thankfully and I was half-way up the stairs when they shouted through the letter-box, 'Al Capone!'

The following day I rang Mr Strega at his office and

told him not to come back to Bianchi's. He was hysterical, threatened to ruin us all; but he remains one of the very few people I have ever barred.

Fortunately most evenings ended on a much merrier note than that, and even though the hours were long I could sit down with the customers when the kitchen shut and enjoy their company. Sometimes they ended with an impromptu sing-song; Jack Elvin, a handsome man who had once modelled for a Players Weights advertisement and was a friend of John Taylor, was a crooner in his cups. He knew all the lyrics of the great standards of the forties and fifties and at the height of the pop craze for mumbling and shouting, it was a pleasure to be reminded of those lovely tunes and actually hear the words for a change. Bill Sirs of the TUC had a beautiful singing voice and there was an evening when a whole crowd of Labour people sang the Red Flag; Aldo and I joined in, rendering it in Italian much to their astonishment, and they made us sing it all over again. That session went on till four in the morning but we all enjoyed it.

Terry Pitt, who was a policy advisor to the Labour Party Council, was at one time a terrible drinker; it was very difficult to get him to go home and just as difficult to persuade a cab-driver to take him. In the end he went on the dry and became an entirely different person. I was so proud of him because I knew it must have taken an enormous effort. Then I didn't see him for some months. I always worried when a customer disappeared, but because Bianchi's was the kind of place used by friends I could usually ask someone for news. One day I asked Lady Wilson, who used to come in with John Betjeman, if she had seen Terry lately and she told me that after giving up the alcohol he had tried to give up smoking, too. He had resorted to nicotine chewing-gum and had choked on a piece in the back of a taxi. It was so sad and seemed the meanest trick of fate to play on a man all set to reform himself.

John Betjeman loved Bianchi's. 'It always feels like coming home,' he would say, and he and Lady Wilson lunched there a lot until he became too ill to manage the stairs. Lady Wilson and I would talk about our families and their progress; she was always interested in everybody and after Sir John's death she came in with her son Giles. I felt I had known him for years as his mother had told me so much about him and we are all still friends. Lady Wilson gave me a book of her poems, another treasured possession, and invited me to go with her to visit Sir John's grave. I couldn't, but I got the impression that she regularly tended it.

Back to the singing. I suppose one of the most glorious moments was accompanying Ella Fitzgerald down the stairs while she sang *A Tisket, a Tasket*, a number she had sung in a film I had seen during the war. She was amazed that anyone could remember it. She had long been my idol and I was excited when I knew she was singing at Ronnie Scott's across the road – but with the hours my customers kept there was no chance of my hearing her and in any case I would have been too shy to go there. But every evening a man booked a table by the window overlooking Ronnie's. His name was Cavallo and he was an American. I couldn't help wondering why, all through his meal, he kept glancing out at the street. We got talking over his order one evening and he asked me if I was really Italian; when I told him yes, he asked what *cavallo* meant in Italian and I said 'horse'. 'You're Italian all right!' he agreed. Then I asked him why he was always looking out of the window and he introduced himself; he was Pete Cavallo, Ella Fitzgerald's road manager, and kept an eye out for her car to arrive so he could nip down the stairs and open the door for her. He said he had told Ella about our marvellous *fettuccini* but she didn't like to eat before the performance. Still, he must have whetted her appetite because one day he rang and asked me if I could bring a tray of it over to Ronnie's. I went to the entrance to hand it over and Pete insisted that I came in and carried it further (I understood what he meant, he liked a sip), so I followed him though it was very dark. He led me backstage, drew aside a curtain and there she was, the great lady herself. I nearly dropped the tray.

'You must be Elena. Pete has told me so much about you.' She lifted the lid from the dish. 'I shouldn't really eat this,' she said and tucked into the lot.

I was thrilled to be in the same room as her and told her so and she promised she would celebrate her birthday at Bianchi's. (I told her my birthday was two days after hers and when it came she sent me orchids.) She was true to her word. She brought her dresser, her bass-player Kita, her pianist Tony Flanagan and Pete, and she insisted I had my photograph taken with her. What a thrill. Jeremy Isaacs was in that evening and asked to be introduced. 'It is an honour to be in the same room as you,' he told her. On her way out I introduced her to my dear friend Melvyn Bragg and his mother, proud and happy to be in a position to do so. She sang *A Tisket, a Tasket* going down the stairs and finished just outside the door into the street. At that moment along came an American couple who hesitated, stared, and said, 'Is it? It can't be!' and when Ella confirmed that it was they were aghast. They lived in New

York and had had to come to Soho to get that close to her. They idolised her too.

I saw her across the road to Ronnie's and she told the doorman that he was to let me in later to hear her. It just happened that it was an evening when Louie was coming to pick me up and take home a crate of wine which I had bought from Mr Petti. When I told him about the invitation he wrinkled his nose. He wasn't into that kind of music. But I put my foot down because I wasn't going to miss out on such a unique opportunity. When we got in the place was packed and we had to stand at the back, but I didn't mind; she was wonderful; the audience loved her and so did Louie. I sneaked a look at his face and it was a treat. 'I think she's fantastic,' was all he could say.

Pete came over to ask us to escort her to her car – which was how Louie came to be introduced. Ella took to him immediately and asked if he would see her to her car every night and he was delighted to do so; it was the beginning of a family friendship that has lasted all these years. Pete writes regularly with all the news and rings whenever they are coming to London.

He called when Ella was appearing at the Albert Hall, saying she wanted to see Louie and Jannette, his wife, but I said it was awkward for them as they had a new baby and it would be difficult for them to get a babysitter at such short notice. He called again the next day, saying that Ella had sent a car round and they had brought Matthew with them; she had sat him on her lap in her dressing-room and sung him a lullaby.

'She usually likes to be on her own before she goes on stage,' he told me, 'but last night she went on truly elated.'

I'm sure the audience thrilled to her performance but

I bet not half as much as I did at the thought of the great Ella Fitzgerald singing to my grandson.

The next time she came to London it was to sing at Grosvenor House and Bob Ringwood, the set designer, came in to say he would like Aldo and me to be his guests as a thank you for looking after him for so many years. It was a sweet gesture. Like many of my customers, when he first came to Bianchi's he was fairly hard-up and we'd go through the menu together planning what he could afford. Now he was successful and could afford to take *us* out. We accepted but I asked if I could bring along Adriana, her husband Brian and Aldo's sister Anselma as my guests, so he booked for us all. Ella didn't know that we were going to be there and I didn't want to disturb her after the cabaret. We were preparing to leave when Kita, the bass-player, spotted us and took us backstage where there were queues of people waiting for her autograph. She was so pleased to see us and introduced us to Nelson Riddle as 'my Italian family in London'. 'Is that your Mafia family?' he joked. I walked her round to the lift and she gave me a hug and a loving kiss. She always made me feel so special.

To an outsider there is something magical about going backstage; it's a self-contained world where everybody has their own job and just gets on with it whether they are actors or stagehands, a bit like the kitchens in restaurants, I suppose, but a bit more glamorous as far as I'm concerned. The first time I went backstage was when Tony Chardet, who had introduced me to Tony Britten all those years ago, invited Louie and myself to see *Hello Dolly* at Drury Lane and took us round before the show to see how it all worked. There was Cameron MacKintosh, the son of one of my customers, sweeping the stage. (He and his friends often came in after the show for whatever was cheapest on the menu.) Tony then took Louie and myself to a box and even gave Louie some chocolates to eat during the show (he was only thirteen then). He accorded us the full VIP treatment, right down to putting us into a taxi afterwards.

Cameron did the same for us all over again many years later when he became a successful impresario himself. He gave us a box to see *Les Misèrables* and had the theatre manager escort us to the VIP room for drinks in the interval; and he has never forgotten that he started backstage.

He gives lots of parties at L'Escargot but the one I remember most was for all the people who had worked with him over the years. In his thank-you speech to them he paid a tribute to me for all the years of friendship. I was out of the room at the beginning of the speech but one of the staff came flying down the stairs to fetch me, he then presented me with a bouquet and I was so touched to be included with his associates I very nearly cried.

Twelve

So many emotions flow round the running of a restaurant; both love and despair get a good airing late at night but I think never more so than on the night Vanessa Redgrave was in with Franco Nero. He was declaring passionate love to her in Italian – and Italians as you know can get very noisy when excited so I could hear every word. They were alone in the place; it was very late and I didn't want to disturb them, so I sat in the other room, not letting him know that I spoke Italian. At the same time I was listening to Marco, one of the waiters, who was threatening to commit suicide, he was so unhappy. Since both parties needed time, we were there till two in the morning. I tried to persuade Marco to go back to Italy where his family would look after him; I was really worried about him because he had made an attempt to kill himself once before. By the time the evening ended two things had been resolved – at least I assume so, as Miss Redgrave later had a child by Nero and Marco did return to Italy.

I have probably talked as many people out of suicide as any Samaritan. I've certainly listened to many cries for help late in the night arising out of situations like that of two male lovers who had been happily together for several years when the older man fell for a young scoundrel. None of their mutual friends liked the new beau and his real lover was heartbroken. He was so distressed one night that Mrs Sydney Nolan asked me what was the matter with him. When I told her she begged me to do all I could to get them back together again. I did my best and eventually succeeded but she, poor dear, was found dead in a hotel room two days later.

I think I helped save Barry Humphries' life once too – not that he was contemplating suicide, but he was genuinely ill. He had come straight off the plane from Australia to meet his old pal Ken Thompson, the press officer for Channel Four. He arrived in his full-length fur coat, delighted to be back, but suddenly complained that he couldn't breathe. He hadn't had a drink for years so I knew it wasn't that kind of jet-lag. I sat him on the stairs and wrapped him in his coat because he was shivering. It was a Saturday lunchtime when quite a few parents brought their children in and one young lad recognised him and told his father to get hold of their doctor. By now we were all very anxious. Barry was stretched out on the floor and I was kneeling beside him holding his hand. Ken was in a state on the phone trying for the doctor. When at last he arrived, he bundled Barry into his car and drove him to a nursing home where he was diagnosed as suffering from complete exhaustion and specifically the effects of hyper-ventilation. Even though he was so ill, as he was helped into the car the people on the street were nodding and winking among themselves as if to say, 'He's had enough.'

A month later he was back, with Ken again, at the same table and I was so happy to see them both – until I turned round and there was Barry stretched out on the floor again. I rushed over and began rubbing his hands and suddenly there was a flash. I looked up and somebody was taking a photograph; when I turned back Barry was on his feet grinning; they had staged the whole thing. I still have the picture and one of the most entertaining things about it is how the people at the next table took absolutely no notice of some poor bugger's total collapse. As far as they were concerned it was my problem, not theirs. Of course, when they discovered who it was they became very excited. I try not to be cynical but some days it is harder than others.

Barry, bless his heart, is still with us. For Christmas 1984 I sent out a card of Dame Edna and myself taken at the launching of one of his books. Over the years, however, I have discovered that the price one pays for having so many friends is the inevitable loss of one of them from time to time. I remember the day James Orr rang me from Buckingham Palace to tell me, 'Your dear friend has passed away.' It was Sir Timothy Bligh. I was invited to his memorial service at St Margaret's Church in Westminster. I had never been to a non-Catholic church before so I was a bit nervous, but I was standing by the pedestrian crossing when Sir Derek and Lady Mitchell found me. 'What are you doing here, Elena?' they asked me, and when I told them they insisted that I come with them to the front instead of hiding away at the back. So there was I surrounded by top politicians, listening to Edward Heath read the lesson and finding myself both surprised and relieved that we all sang the same hymns.

Over the years I have received many letters from bereaved families which I find very touching and considerate – I am able to avoid making tactless enquiries and am made to feel like part of their family. I am also cushioned from the kind of shock I had one lunchtime when John Hurt rang to say he was coming in with a whole group of friends and they might be a little bit late. I could hear a lot of jollity going on in the background. I set about calculating who would be leaving early and making a mental plan of tables. Even though they had phoned, nothing quite prepared me for their arrival.

There was Jilly Conyers carrying an enormous bunch of camelias, Jeremy Brett, John Morgan, Maria Aitken, Lord Harlech, Brian Rix, Denholm and Susie Elliot and Diana Rigg. As I was organising putting the tables together Jilly asked if I had any candles; when I replied that I hadn't, she laid the flowers down the centre of the table. I thought perhaps it was a wedding celebration. The flowers took up a lot of room and I suggested putting them on the floor.

'Oh, no, they are for D'Arcy. He always loved coming here.'

And that was how I learned my great friend D'Arcy Conyers, her husband had died. They had come straight from the funeral. I was tremendously shocked; he had been in late one night only the week before, with an opera singer – so late that all I could provide was spaghetti *al dente* – and he had been in sparkling form and stayed till about two. I knew Jilly was being very brave – she was suddenly a widow with a small daughter to bring up alone – but I wished somebody had told me. I was shattered.

But life must go on and it was a great pleasure for me to be part of the rebirth of a very talented man's career. It all happened so sweetly and simply. There was a young man who came in often – Stefan Andke, who worked for a Swedish publishing house. One day he introduced me to his grandfather, who was a charming old man.

'Will you be my grandfather, too? I never had one,'

I asked him, and from then on I always addressed him as 'Grandfather' which he never minded. One day he said he was going to the ballet and showed me his tickets for the gods.

'But surely Stefan could have got you better seats,' I said.

'I got them myself,' he replied. 'When I was young, people climbed up into the gods to see me; I can do the same now to see the people I admire.' He said no more as at that moment Stefan came to collect him. It was his last night in London.

A few weeks later Stefan came in with a small booklet of paintings and drawings saying that Grandfather (I found out later they were friends, not relatives) had written asking him to give them to me. They were by a man called Einer Nerman and, though I was very pleased that he had thought of me, the name meant nothing. I kept the book in my handbag and on Grandfather's next visit to London thanked him and asked him to sign it for me. The signature said 'Einer Nerman'. I was impressed that he had been an artist but it still meant little to me until I showed the book to Ken Thompson and Charles Osborne the theatre critic. They wanted to meet him at once but Grandfather had already gone back to Sweden. However, I had his address and Ken and Sandy Wilson went off to Scandinavia to find him. The following year they produced a book and an exhibition of Grandfather's work. Apparently he had been a celebrated theatre cartoonist in the twenties and thirties who had been introduced to London society by Ivor Novello, who had met him in 1918. He had actually come to London as a ballet dancer on a variety bill at the Coliseum but had baulked at the idea of touring and had taken some drawings to the *Tatler* who engaged him immediately. He stayed with them for ten years sketching, so very wittily, every major star of the period. He then went on to America and Hollywood before retiring to Sweden. When his exhibition opened and his book was published here the *Daily Telegraph Magazine* gave him a great spread – and he drew John Gielgud again after fifty years. He told me that meeting me had given him a new lease of life; he had been forgotten for so many years. I could not have chosen a better grandfather.

Thirteen

Soho has always attracted journalists and Mr Bianchi worried when the new fashionable *trattorias* opened to so much publicity in the late sixties. I told him there was bound to be a certain amount of dropping out at first, because it was part of the job to explore such places, but they would be writing about us again soon. I was right; we had too many important customers for the gossip columnists to ignore. They may have been rivals in print but Nigel Dempster, Peter McKay, Paul Callan, Richard Ingrams and the rest were all great friends and would frequently come in and squeeze round a table; what they talked about I don't know, but they laughed a lot.

There were other sorts of correspondent too – people like Murray Sayle, Nick Tomalin of the *Sunday Times* and Anthony Summers from the BBC. I remember Anthony arriving late for lunch with Nick in a fluster because he had accidentally wrenched the door off a taxi. How on earth could he have done that, we all wanted to know. 'It was all so stupid. I'd given him the name of the street and when he pulled in he slowed down and asked if this was all right. I said Bianchi's was a couple of doors up but that would be OK – but as I opened the door he moved up and the door caught on a lamppost and came clean off its hinges. He was a nice man, one of the best drivers I've ever had. I gave him my address because he said he might have some trouble with his insurance.'

And with that they settled down to enjoy their lunch. A few days later Tony was sent to Vietnam for a couple of months and, as he said on his welcome return, had quite forgotten the incident. The taxi driver on the other hand had not and had been bombarding his secretary with angry phone calls, followed by calls from his solicitor. It had gone so far that Tony had to go to his own solicitor who was sure they were just trying it on. They weren't. The whole thing ended up in court where the judge, after listening to both sides, concluded with: '. . . and Mr Summers admits he was in a hurry to go to Bianchi's, a restaurant notable in London as a meeting place and watering hole for journalists. Given the nature of the rendezvous I have decided to find in favour of the taxi driver.'

I was most indignant – fancy calling us a watering-hole – but it cost poor Tony almost £200 in legal fees and when you consider you could have a meal for two for £2, top whack, in the old days, that was a lot of money.

Ron Hall was also part of Tony's group and it was he who organised a farewell party for Murray Sayle when he was sent to Japan as the *Sunday Times* Far East correspondent. On the night, Ron Hall came in to cancel the party because Murray had flu but asked if we could have it instead the following week. When Nick Tomalin came tearing in thinking he was late – he had been working from home and nobody had thought to tell him the party was off – he called Claire, his wife, and suggested they went to the pictures instead. While he was waiting for her I sat and had a drink with him, something I very seldom did at the beginning of the evening. He was carrying a little boat with a gun carriage on top and I thought it was a present for one of his children, but he told me it was a momento for Murray who was one of our finest war correspondents. He asked me to take care of it until the next week; then Claire arrived and off they went.

In a matter of days, Nick was sent to cover the Yom Kippur War in Israel and the party had to be postponed again. I tucked the little gun-boat away safely but the party never took place. Nick was killed by a heat-seeking missile on the Golan Heights. His colleagues knew how much I loved Nick and came in to see me; I told them about his gift to Murray and they promised to send it on to him – but it was very painful to part with it.

Journalists and writers do lead strange lives and they have introduced some strange people into the restaurant from time to time. Two boys – dancers from *Carte Blanche* at the Phoenix – brought a Dutch journalist in whenever he was in London. One evening they booked a table for four saying their friend Willem Oltman was flying in from New York with a man he was interviewing. The man seemed incredibly nervous after the flight so I helped him choose a light meal of soup and veal marsala; in fact I made so much fuss of him the boys jokingly accused me of flirting. Willem asked me to order a car to the Hilton for him. Because he was a stranger I said I would see him out myself.

'We don't want you getting into the wrong car and ending up in the wrong place,' I said cheerfully and he looked jumpier than ever.

The next day the boys told me that he had been a friend of Lee Harvey Oswald, the man who shot President Kennedy, and Willem was trying to get his story.

It was difficult as the man kept clamming up, so Willem proposed they went to a secret hideaway in Holland. He never got there. The boys told me he had disappeared on his way to Willem's Dutch office and had been found shot dead in Miami a few days later, supposedly having committed suicide.

Journalists can sometimes be economical with the truth without realising the trouble and anger their stories are going to cause. I had to ring Bill Heseltine at Buckingham Palace the day they spread the story that Princess Diana had wept at L'Escargot. It wasn't even remotely true but I had to ring to tell him I had not put the story about, nor had any of my staff. Of course he trusted and believed me and went so far as to send me a letter confirming this, but it was distressing and Princess Diana did not return.

On the other hand journalists can take up the cudgels against injustice very powerfully – which is what Peter Watson did for another customer of mine, Harry Calleia, when he was with the *Sunday Times*. Harry often ate with his friend and business associate Garry Garbon and Garry's girlfriend Betty, and one year he lent them his car to go on holiday to Algeria. He came in one day saying he was worried because he had received a telegram from them saying they had had an accident and Betty was in hospital and he was flying out there to see how he could help. The next thing we heard was not only that he had been arrested as a drugs smuggler – something Aldo and I were sure he was not – but that he had been sentenced to death by firing squad. I told Peter that Harry was a dear friend and customer and he said he would look into it. He gave the case a lot of publicity, revealing that the telegram had been sent by the Algerian drugs squad when Garry and Betty were already under arrest. He also revealed that Harry had been kept in solitary confinement and had been horribly tortured, having had parts of his toes cut away.

The publicity eventually gained Harry his freedom and he came to Bianchi's to thank us for our indirect help. He was flat broke so we offered to stand him a meal but he shook his head; he was a man not only physically damaged by his experience but broken in spirit too. He told us he still had his boat and was going to get on it and let it take him to wherever it would – and we never saw or heard from him again.

We had our own brush with the law and drugs one evening when four men and a woman came in. The restaurant was crowded and I was about to tell them they would have to wait when they flashed their identity cards; they were from the drugs squad and wanted to search the premises. Well, flabbergasted wasn't the word for it, but I said as long as they didn't disturb my customers they could look where they liked. They started pulling out every drawer in the servery and they found my big tin of paracetemol that I kept for customers if they had a headache, also the small tin I used to take to the table. I told them what they were but they ummed and aahed, convinced they had stumbled across a great cache of dope. They demanded my handbag which was in a drawer under the cash register. As Aldo went to open the drawer he was suddenly told to 'freeze' and put his hands up. Perhaps they thought we kept a gun in there or something. So there was poor Aldo sitting with his hands above his head and Mr Ricci, one of the owners, asking me in Italian what the hell was going on. I replied in English – I wasn't going to get caught for conspiring to abort the course of justice or whatever it's called. Eventually they agreed that the tablets were not anything sinister and trooped off down the stairs. We were all a bit shaken but then we started to laugh at the memory of Aldo looking like something out of a film on telly. In all my years in Soho, that (apart from sacking a couple of waiters because they smoked pot) is the nearest I have come to anything to do with drugs.

Never been involved with the Mafia either, though I did have a few qualms when Gerry Wilson the screenwriter, whom I've known for over twenty years, rang me to ask if it would be all right to bring in this American hit-man whose story he was going to turn into a film. I knew I could trust Gerry so I booked them a table; well, if I'd had a few qualms over the phone it was nothing to the quakes I felt when they arrived. The man was six feet seven inches tall and must have weighed over twenty stone; he also had a full beard and looked like something out of the old Wild West. Gerry's not exactly tiny either and if they had said they were from the Mafia I think everyone in the room would have handed over their money instantly. The man's name was Papa Forenson and he was famous as a bounty-hunter – what you might call a super-bailiff who gets sent after people who have jumped bail – in America, where the people who are owed money do not care whether the debtor is returned to them dead or alive. I shuddered to think of some of my poor customers in their hard-up times.

It didn't take many visits to see how he kept up that enormous size; he just worked his way through the menu and washed it down with anything up to five bottles of wine. Gerry told me later that he had given up the project after three weeks, deciding it would mean either his liver or his life. Somebody else wrote the film which was called *The Bounty Hunter* and was Steve McQueen's last film.

Gerry told me that the man was incredibly gentle, never swore, was a preacher in a Californian church, an astrologist who wouldn't leave the house if the stars were wrong, and a philanthropist who ran a home for reformed gangsters in California. Papa Forenson's stories may have been unbelievable but they were true. Like the time he tracked a man down to a bar in a small town where the debt was to be paid and the man did a runner into the gents where he had an accomplice waiting to stick a flick-knife into his pursuer. It must have been a bit like a Popeye cartoon when Papa Forenson didn't flinch and pulled a gun on them. They just fainted and were taken in unconscious. I could well understand their feelings.

There were similar odd happenings closer to home, both in the restaurant and in the streets around. Two strangers came in one day – great big chaps they were – who told me they were looking for someone; well I didn't like the look of them at all and told them that the guests of all the hosts had arrived, nobody was waiting for them, a deliberate way of misunderstanding them. Alan Hargreaves, who at the time was working on *Thames at Six* on television, saw them standing over me in a most intimidating fashion and left his table to offer help. They took one look at him and decided to leave. I never did find out who they were or who they were looking for. On another occasion a man came in enquiring about a customer. I don't know why but I was immediately suspicious of him, especially when he asked if I would sit down and talk to him which I obviously couldn't do as I was far too busy; but I said he could come back after lunch. He took some money out of his wallet and offered it to me. I refused it. I was quite shocked. I asked him his name but he wouldn't give it to me. He didn't return – for which I was very thankful. The person he had been asking about wrote for the *Observer* and at that time quite a few journalists received threats from the various organisations they were investigating.

Not all of the mysteries surrounded strangers, of course. There was a man who for years came in with his wife – a respectable man, a government official or civil servant, charming and well-bred. Then to my utter surprise one of his cheques bounced and I didn't see him for ages. Eventually he started to use the restaurant again, but now he was always with boys, young boys. I said nothing when he first offered me a cheque again but this time it didn't bounce and he became a regular once more – until, that is, he was found stabbed to death in his Kensington home. There was much speculation in the papers that he may have been a member of MI6 (which could well have been true, given his complete about-turn sexually), but I think he was far more likely to have been murdered for money by one of his pickups.

Fourteen

As society became more and more 'permissive' the streets round Soho reflected the change; the illegal bookies had gone and the porno men and the amusement arcades were moving in and making a lot of money, the sort of money that was bound to lead to trouble – as it did one evening in Old Compton Street. We all knew Tony Zomparelli, he was an acquaintance of Mr Petti, Mr Bianchi's accountant. I saw Tony after lunch as I was leaving for my break; I think he was on his way up to the office to see Charlie Petti. I saw him again on my return to work; Tony and Charlie were talking outside the barber's shop in Frith Street. I said goodnight to them and they walked together down to the postbox on the corner of Dean Street where they parted – Mr Petti to fetch his car and Tony to turn back into Old Compton Street. Half an hour later Jeremy Brett came in with his son David and a schoolfriend, and said something awful had happened in Old Compton Street. He didn't know what as he had hurried the boys past but there seemed to be police and ambulances everywhere. I heard during the evening that there had been a shooting outside the amusement arcade, but it wasn't until I read the morning papers that I found out it was poor Tony. Apparently when I saw him he had been trying to borrow money from Mr Petti who had refused him.

The amusement arcade stands where Chez Auguste used to be. Chez Auguste was next door to the Café Bleu and was an elegant French restaurant from the Edwardian days with a banqueting hall at the back that is now Ronnie Scott's Club. When it became an arcade full of mindless games, the Café Bleu was replaced by a shop selling spanking magazines. And all the time the near-beer rip-off clubs were flourishing. These are the places where out-of-towners go hoping to find a bit of the Soho action; usually the only action they find comes when the bouncers threaten to throw them out for refusing to pay the astronomical price asked for a couple of cokes and a chat with a 'hostess' – who drinks near-champagne and promises the stranger the experience of a lifetime after she has finished work. Mostly, after a bit of bluster about calling the police, the poor dupes pay up and leave.

One night I heard a terrible commotion in the street – a woman screaming blue murder – and I looked out of the window thinking it might be a genuine attack, which in a way it was. A victim of the near-beer place up the street had waited outside for his promised lady who when she emerged from her shift had doubtless told him where to go in a sentence of two words. For once the victim bit back, literally; he bit her bum and she was dancing all over the street. I'm sure it was very painful but it was also very funny.

There was a lady who gave better value for money who lived next door to Bianchi's; we all knew of her existence; I once had to direct a man with a white stick to her premises. He had come up the stairs of Bianchi's and was heading for the upper floors when I pointed out his mistake and led him next door. I stood at the bottom of the stairs and saw a lady in a black silk slip come out to welcome him; he was obviously a regular. Then one night, just as Giorgio (the waiter who always walked me to the late-night bus stop) and I were closing the restaurant, the phone rang. The man on the other end sounded very agitated and begged me to take a message next door to the... er... prostitute, to tell her that her son was very ill in France and that she must ring him at the number he gave me urgently as he was going away the following day. Of course, I said 'yes'. Giorgio was in a lather of anxiety at the prospect of my going next door as there was a Maltese gambling club on the first floor and the proprietors certainly weren't going to welcome my presence on their premises. But I knew I had to do it, family is family. I marched past the door to the club and several came running out. I told them I had a message for Madame but they said she had gone home. I left a little note explaining all and hurried back to the safety of Bianchi's.

That's how I found out that the ladies of the street only rented their flats for the daytime. They slipped off home to the suburbs each evening, probably looking like any respectable shopgirl after a hard day's work at a department store, or even, come to that, like a waitress – although I was only once mistaken for a street-walker. (I was standing out on the pavement waiting to see a customer out and the girls came rushing across the street saying I was not one of them.)

The day after I had taken her the message Madame sent me a note saying please would I visit her. The invitation shocked Mr Bianchi but I said I must go to find out if her son was all right. The flat was beautiful – though you would never have guessed from the stairway – and she had laid out lunch with fine china and glass, flowers everywhere. She didn't understand the late-night phone-call because she had no son. It was all most mysterious – and I never saw her again.

The one I have seen constantly over the years, and oh so sadly, is Spanish Betty. I have known her since Café Bleu days when she used to have a beat in Shaftesbury Avenue. She was known as Madame Adelina – to her face at least – and would book a table for herself and her maid. She followed Piero, Mr Petti's partner, to Bianchi's after the fire and we became quite friendly. She was always talking about her daughter whom she had sent away to be educated in France, and one day she arranged a party for the girl's homecoming with masses of flowers and a huge cake. The girl never turned up which was heart-breaking for her mother.

Spanish Betty became very friendly with our waiter Giorgio – in fact a bit too friendly in that she became very demanding. Giorgio would take her poodle to the beauty parlour for a trim and shampoo, then the dog would be sent home by taxi. What a performance! She would also use Giorgio as her escort to film and theatre premières, which were very glamorous affairs then. I don't think she knew the stars but she probably knew the movie moguls quite well as their offices were right on her doorstep in Wardour Street. Then things began to go wrong and she kept on at Giorgio to bring me round to her flat as she wanted to sell a mink jacket. I didn't want it and I certainly wasn't going to try and sell it to any of my customers so I put off going there for as long as I could. Also, although Soho was tolerant of whatever people did to earn their living I knew that a respectable young woman like myself was not expected to visit a prostitute at home. Eventually I gave in (though without saying a word to Mr Bianchi or

Aldo) and we clambered up the rickety stairs to her flat and her maid opened the door.

Inside it was unbelievable: all in white with diamond-shaped padded-leather cladding on doors and furniture, flowers everywhere, a huge glass-topped white table, and silver-framed pictures of herself as young woman all over the place. She was dressed in a negligée and handed me a glass of brandy large enough for my head to fall in. It was so grand I promptly got the giggles, especially when the doorbell rang and the maid went to the hall to negotiate. So this is how the other half lives was all I could think. She showed me her bedroom which was as opulent as a film set – again a white padded-leather dressing-table, wardrobe too and a huge bed. I realised it was probably the cheap stick-on stuff but it did look grand in a thoroughly tarty way. Anyhow, she accepted that I wasn't going to buy the mink and we were ushered out while the unknown gentleman was ushered in by another door.

Giorgio and I couldn't stop laughing at our adventure, though we didn't say a word about it when we got back to work. We were very good friends, still are; he was gay and it helped him to have someone to talk to; he couldn't have told his parents. When he went back to Milan he gave Aldo and myself a book of early filmstars with all our favourites in it. He lived in the States for a while and we met up on our last trip over there. He is in Milan again now and doing very well – which is more than can be said for poor Spanish Betty. I met her in the street not long ago with her feet and hands so swollen she could hardly move along the pavement. She told me she was homeless (she had been swindled out of her flat by a young tart and her pimp) and I got the impression she was living in a hostel. She begged me to give her a job at L'Escargot but I couldn't – with those hands she wasn't even capable of doing the washing up – but I felt bad about refusing her.

Not that all the women who lived in Soho were on the game. Annie Ross and Georgia Brown shared a flat in Old Compton Street when they were setting out on their singing careers, and there were quite a few theatrical seamstresses who lived and worked round about. The flats were cheap then and so were the shops – you could buy anything from a pair of hand-stitched gloves to half a pound of salami without having to do more than cross the road. Mrs Pike, a magistrate from Sussex, shared a flat above Bifulco the butcher (now yet another T-shirt shop), on the corner of Frith Street and Old Compton Street, with her widowed sister Mrs Firth. She told me that they only used the place as a *pied-à-terre* for going to the theatre or occasional entertaining and asked me whether I knew someone who would like to live there permanently. As it happened Alex, one of the waiters, was looking for a place so he moved in. This cemented our friendship with Mrs Pike which led in turn to one of the most delightful weekends Aldo and I ever spent.

It started as quite a lot of things do in Soho with an absolute disaster: the kitchen downstairs at Bianchi's caught fire. A pan of fat burst into flames and although the staff tried hard they couldn't put it out. The restaurant was full and smoke was filtering up the stairs and people were making remarks like, 'I know I ordered my steak well done, but don't you think the chef is overdoing it, Elena?' I rang down and could hear chaos so I asked everyone to leave, telling them there was a small fire in the kitchen. Nobody moved, they all thought it was a bit of a joke. Gray Jolliffe the cartoonist said, 'I've just come from the preview of *Towering Inferno* and this is only a fire in a basement! In any case, I ordered smoked salmon so that should be all right.' I kept on at them to go but it was a Friday lunchtime and they were all quite relaxed. It wasn't until the chef came bounding up the stairs, his hair and clothes singed by the flames and the smoke billowing out behind him, that we all realised just how serious it was. But funnily enough, though perhaps not surprisingly, everyone grabbed all the bottles off the tables before they fought their way down the stairs which were now pitch black with smoke.

Outside the customers held an impromptu street party. There was Georgie Fame, who was on the receiving end of comments about his song *You've Left Your Blue Flame*; Malcolm McDowell; Graham Cornthwaite, a photographer who now lives in Rome; John O'Donnell, an advertising man; and Mai Zetterling – who had left her coat behind and had to catch a plane. I fought my way upstairs and rescued it from table 15. The chief fireman came with me but I had to go because I was the only one who knew where to find it.

With those kind of names involved the incident made the evening news. Ken Thompson was the first one round to see if I was all right; oddly enough he had been to a friend's wedding reception at L'Escargot Bienvenu, as it was then called, and he very sweetly took a picture of me in the empty restaurant, which was quite unscathed. It was a very reassuring act; I would be back.

Major Pike, Mrs Pike's husband also heard the news and when I got home there was a firm invitation for Aldo and me to come and spend the weekend as their guests; after the madness of the day it was a pleasure to accept. They sent a car to fetch us and courteously mentioned that they always dressed for dinner. They lived in a large country house and had made the effort to invite people we knew as customers (I managed to restrain myself from picking up the plates at the end of the meal).

The following morning we set off for drinks at the home of one of their neighbours. He was a lord who sometimes accompanied Mrs Pike to the opera, so I'd met him but had no idea how grand he was. He was tremendously hospitable and welcoming but I do remember feeling a bit stunned when his wife announced that she had to go to see to the roast as it was the butler's day off. A very different life from mine.

Then it was back into the car to be taken to meet some other neighbours for more drinks. It was another grand house but this time owned by people who had made their money in the City – *nouveau riche* – and there our reception was decidedly snotty. The hostess could hardly contain her disdain at the thought of having a waitress from Soho under her roof, though her guests, yet again titled persons, were fascinated by the idea of Soho and wanted to know all about it. I suppose it didn't fit in with the lady of the manor's idea of social climbing but it made Aldo and me feel uncomfortable – goodness knows we were out of our depth already. The major was very quick to sense this and rescued us, saying that lunch would be ready at home. His language was decidedly Army as he put his foot down on the accelerator. He was furious that friends of his should have been slighted and, bless him, he was also proof that money can't buy you class.

Fifteen

The fire that shut down Bianchi's for three weeks was not the first one there; several years before the food-lift shaft had caught alight. It happened one lunchtime when Kika Markham and some other actors were in a hurry to get back to rehearsals. I sent their order down to the kitchens and when the bell rang to inform me that the food was on its way up I opened the dumb-waiter in the servery. I was appalled when smoke came belching out. From then on it was a madhouse; the fire had started half-way up the lift and so as I was chucking buckets of water down it the chef, unaware of the problem, was hollering up it thinking I had gone barmy or something. Every time he tried to load the lift shaft he got drenched. I dialled 999 but the fire engines went to Fleet Street by mistake and by the time they arrived I had put the fire out myself and with the waiters was running up and down three flights of stairs to serve the food. The firemen told me it had been caused by a faulty switch and I was lucky to be alive as the water could have conducted the electrical current back to me. Fortunately I always fix rubber soles to my shoes and they were apparently what saved me. I was a bit shaken but no one was late for rehearsals.

    I have been very lucky in the friendships I have made with my customers. In many cases they span three generations. Nina and Richard Lowry are now both High

Court judges and grandparents and we often remember the evening I had to run down the street after Richard as he had left behind the beautiful heart-shaped box of chocolates he had bought for Nina as a Christmas present before they were married. Since then all anniversaries and birthdays have been celebrated at Bianchi's. We have shared pictures and stories of our children, mutually proud of their progress. Aldo and I were invited to their daughter Emma's twenty-first birthday party in the Middle Temple – which was quite nostalgic for us as we had played in the gardens when we were children – and Judge Nina wrote, when their son Stephen was to be married at the Gray's Inn Chapel, 'that no family occasion would be complete' without us. It was typically thoughtful of her.

Watching romances grow into lasting love is always a warming experience. Anthony Andrews first came to Bianchi's when he was in his teens; then he started to bring Georgina in and I saw their love blossom into marriage. It was the same with Jeremy Irons and Sinead Cusack. Both couples still come to L'Escargot to see me and I love to know they are still happy. I have seen many matches made.

Love can take any number of forms but I think the truest and dearest version I ever saw was in the case of a couple who had been married for six years. They came in one evening and he told me that although she was leaving him for another man, in appreciation of the six beautiful years they had had together he was paying for dinner. He fussed over what she was eating because she was already pregnant by her new lover. Not long after that I learned the new lover was out of the picture – something I'd rather expected, I'm afraid. Her by-then-ex-husband was wonderful; he offered her a flat in his

With my family celebrating forty years in Soho

With Aldo and Ella Fitzgerald

With Melvyn Bragg

Myself with Mrs John Logie Baird at Bianchi's

Myself with Dame Edna

With Lady Wilson

With Aldo at L'Escargot

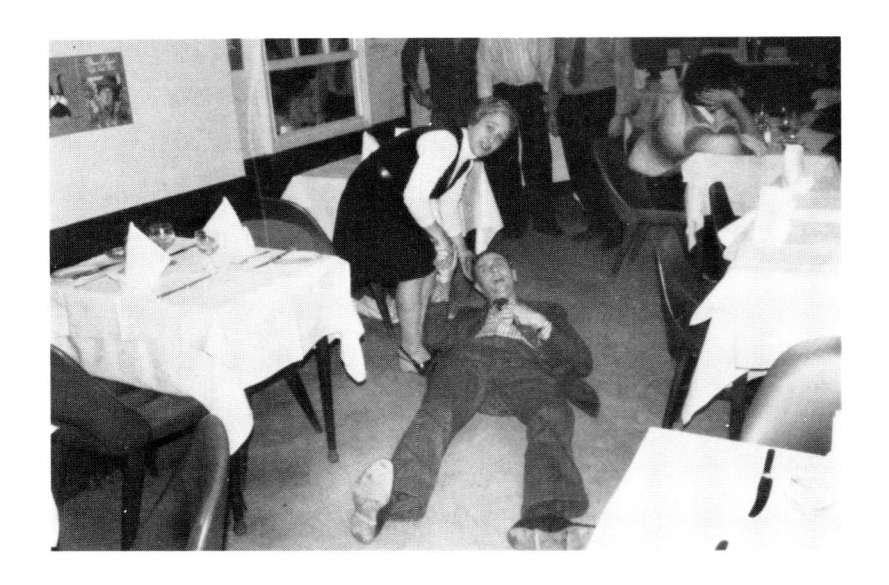

Barry Humphries pulling my leg

With Arnold Saltzman

At Bianchi's (*The Hulton Picture Company*)

My grandchildren (l. to r.) Tomas, Simon, Matthew, Justin and Jamie

house, helped her through the birth of her son and shared the babysitting. He adored the child because it was hers. Tragically the mother died of a brain tumour when the boy was five years old but the ex-husband adopted him and raised him as his own. They now live in France but he still writes to me. I find that level of love very touching.

I have received many touching gifts too, one of them in an absurdly comic incident. I noticed a customer, Paul Arden from the advertising business, bent down over the table holding his napkin to his mouth. I went over to see what was the matter.

'I think I've lost a filling from my tooth,' he mumbled.

I pushed his bowl of *moules marinière* to one side and said, 'Let's have a look.' He unfolded the napkin and there was a tiny silvery grey object in the middle. 'It's a pearl from the mussels,' I told him.

He didn't believe me. He rolled his tongue round his mouth to check whether there were any gaps and wrapped the tiny stone in a tissue. I laughed and told him that mussels made pearls just like oysters and finally he was convinced. He finished his meal well pleased that he hadn't got to spend the afternoon at the dentist. I thought nothing more of it until he came in just before Easter.

'I've got a present for you, Elena,' and he gave me a little box. Inside there was a beautiful little scarf-pin with the mussel pearl set in the centre. 'I took it to a jeweller's and you were right.'

'But you ought to give it to your wife,' I protested.

'No, it came from you and she wants you to have it, too.' It was lovely and I wear it to this day.

Another piece of jewellery I treasure began with a

gift from Sir Charles Rothschild; he gave me a £50 note for Christmas with the instruction that I was to buy myself something special – and for once, instead of ploughing it back into the family, I decided to do just that. Other customers had been generous too, bless them, and I had about £200 to spend. I went to Charlie Petti, Mr Bianchi's partner (and the only one of my bosses I ever called by his first name), the very same person from whom I had bought broken wafers for a halfpenny when I was a kid, because he also now had a jewellery business. He found me the perfect memento, a little gold heart set with diamonds and on a chain; as soon as I saw it I knew it was just what I wanted; something by which to remember everyone.

My walls at home are covered with framed souvenirs, among them a very funny poem by Dippy Diplock referring to the fact that his crowd drank a lot and used bad language; he presented it to me when he celebrated his twenty-fifth wedding anniversary. There is a collection of cartoonists autographs given to me on my last night at Bianchi's, April the first, of course. I had intended to leave the week before but stayed on just for their benefit as they had held their annual reunion at Bianchi's for so many years.

Then there is a copy of an article Philip Kleinman wrote in the *Sunday Times* after we had a fight with the Weights and Measures people over our long-stemmed carafes. Some EEC ruling had made them illegal because they contained slightly less than the regulation bottle; it was decreed that only bottles could be served. This upset the customers so much they looked into the law themselves and discovered that it said only that all containers must arrive at the table 'with the cork in place' – so we promptly put corks in the carafes and the place looked like home again. It was such a triumph that everyone wanted to autograph the article and there it hangs in my hall with the signatures of Peter Cook, Kingsley and Martin Amis, Sandy Gall, Ian McKellen, Albert Finney and Richard Ingrams.

Tucked away upstairs in a drawer are three scripts by Henry Livings given to Aldo because they used to sit and chat together. Henry still writes to us; once a postcard even came to tell us he had survived a small operation on his balls. I just hoped the postman hadn't found time to read it.

I have albums full of photographs, too, and some are of particular interest. John Logie Baird had invented television in the house that became Bianchi's and we had a plaque commemorating this in the large room. One day a customer brought in a very handsome woman whom he introduced as Mrs John Logie Baird, over on a visit from South Africa. She was very touched by the fact that her husband had not been forgotten. I am especially proud of the pictures I have of us together. I didn't tell her the story of the phone-call taken on a certain occasion by one of my staff who didn't speak very good English. I could hear her repeating to a customer on the other end, 'But we don't have bedrooms.' The poor man was trying to book a table in the Baird Room and she, young enough to take television for granted, had no idea that it had been invented only a few feet from where she was sitting.

Not all memories get recorded so some I have to carry in my head; like of the day Susannah York, who was playing Peter Pan at the Prince Edward Theatre, came in for a quick snack. There was a little boy, about six, having lunch with his parents and grandparents before going to see the show. I told him she sometimes came in here to eat. He was most indignant, insisting that Peter Pan was a boy. At that moment Susannah arrived, dressed for the show but with a cloak over her costume. I asked her to show him she was really Peter Pan and when she did you should have seen his little face, it was a treat.

As I've said, parents often brought their children in for Saturday lunch and a particularly funny occasion was when Graham Terry came in with his son Christopher. The boy wanted fish-fingers and Graham looked at me appalled. I nodded very seriously to Christopher, winked at Graham and served the boy *sole goujons* – which he scoffed happily, convinced they were fish-fingers. Another satisfied customer.

Being able to help customers out has always been very much part of the job to me; I've got to know so many people over the years, and it does help if you can mention somebody's name so that when a phone-call comes it will be expected, and everyone knows me well enough now to respect my judgement. Goodness knows, I've had to learn the hard way and often by looking a little foolish at first; never mind – I learn quickly.

One day Anne Jackson the actress came in and said she was waiting for her husband and wanted to introduce him. I said I'd be delighted to meet him and I meant it because she is a very fine lady. Afterwards I went back to the servery and Aldo said, 'Look who's here.'

I said, 'Yes, that's Mr Jackson.'

'No, it's not, that's Eli Walach.'

I was most indignant. 'I've just been introduced and Anne told me herself he was her husband.'

'It's still Eli Walach, the filmstar.'

Of course Aldo was right, but to me he was just a nice man who was her husband.

Then Cis Yudkin came in with another American couple and they all seemed to know each other and Cis told me that the people wanted to borrow her flat in Harley Street to give a party, could I help out with the arrangements? I suggested that champagne would be easier than getting in a whole load of spirits and mixers; they agreed, and I went round myself to French Lou at the Vintage House to get the booze delivered and hire the glasses. It all went very smoothly and the wife rang me on the Sunday to thank me. She had told me her name but the penny didn't drop until I saw Cis again and she said that the husband was Alger Hiss, one of the first men to go to prison for un-American activities at the direction of Senator Joe McCarthy and Richard Nixon. I was glad to have been able to help a man who had gone through such a terrible ordeal.

As I said earlier, I learn quickly and when he came back to London I recognised him at once. He was having lunch with his publisher and by a curious coincidence Anne Jackson was lunching in the other room. I told Alger Hiss Anne was in and he went across to say hello. Neither of them knew the other was in London. Sitting at a nearby table was Frank Czitanovich, who also knew Anne. Frank called me over to ask about the man talking to Anne. I told him who it was and Frank said he had just come from a meeting about making a programme on Hiss. So although I sometimes don't recognise people I can still bring them together.

Sixteen

In the late seventies Soho began to change yet again. It had become very seedy with far too many sex shops and cinemas and was no longer the place where families with small children could shop happily. So the Soho Society and the Westminster Council got together to limit the numbers and the displays of such places. It was a hard fight to clean up Soho and some of the results were not foreseen by the campaigners; the closure of many long-established shops like Parmagina and Bifulco, on the corners of Old Compton Street, and Delmonico the wine merchant. They went because the crafty porno dealers had smelled the wind of change and invested in property while the area was still run down. When the leases came up for re-negotiation small shops could no longer afford the overheads. It was sad.

There were changes taking place at Bianchi's, too. When Mr Bianchi retired Charlie Petti took over the restaurant with a new partner, Nino Ricci. There were many people queueing to buy the place (Mike Luckwell from the Moving Picture Company for one, who planned to give me shares) but my loyalty was still with my Italian–Soho connections and I stayed on as manageress, even though dear old Charlie was getting past it; his memory was going so Aldo was looking after the accounts as cashier.

All was fine for a while until Mr Ricci introduced his

nineteen-year-old son, Piero Luigi, into the business. Now I am very adaptable and had been to school with his mother, so I made allowances for his lack of knowledge until two incidents occurred. The first was when Jeremy Isaacs, a regular and much-liked customer arrived late one night. I had heard on the grapevine that he was getting the Channel Four job and knew that he had been held up at a meeting. I told him that all I could organise was some minestrone and some cheese and that was fine by him; he was never, ever demanding or commanding. But it wasn't fine by Piero Luigi who took me to one side and told me that I was never to do that again – that is, go down to the kitchen myself to serve a customer who had arrived after the official closing time. I was choked; to be told off by a kid after all my years in the business was infuriating, but I kept my counsel.

The second incident happened on New Years Eve 1978 when David Bell, then the Head of Entertainment for LWT, came in late to wish me a Happy New Year. David told me he had had the utmost difficulty getting past Piero, who had insisted the place was closed; he couldn't understand why he should try to prevent him from delivering his good wishes. I began to brood about my job and my future; I couldn't bear the thought that all my years of loyalty and love towards my customers were to be ruined by that boy's attitude; didn't he realise that these people were his bread and butter? I got to wondering why I was working six days a week for employers who did not even value their customers. It was hard to accept they were not my kind, especially when I had worked with friends all my life. The Riccis went off to Grosvenor House to celebrate New Year, and Aldo and I had to walk back home to Islington through black-iced roads as there was a four-hour wait for cabs. Nobody had thought to book one for us. Bitterness, an alien emotion to me, entered my life.

I was no longer really happy at my work though I still loved all my customers. Some of them guessed what was going on – after all we had been friends and confidantes for years – but the last straw came when Mr and Mrs Ricci went on holiday. While they were away their son threw a party at their house for the younger members of the staff on a Saturday night. On the Monday Mr Petti called me and asked me if I had taken a case of wine from the store, and I told him no, as we hadn't been busy and in any case I would have signed for it if I had; after thirty years I knew the routine. He buzzed downstairs to see if the manager had taken it and the reply was the same. When his parents returned Piero Luigi told his father he had been accused of stealing. Mr Ricci assembled the staff and asked if anyone had taken it, and they all denied all knowledge; there was absolutely no mention of the party. I looked at them hard but there was no shaming them. I was furious so I turned to Mr Ricci and said, 'Would you like to call the police and send them to my house to search it? Aldo is at home and I will stay here so that you can see that I don't call him and tell him to hide it, and when you have done that I will call my lawyer.' I could have told him where I guessed it had gone, but I wasn't having that little brat ruin my honour.

Within a few days I handed in my notice. I was sixty years old, I had worked all my life and for the first time I was not enjoying it. The reaction was typical.

'If you leave I shall have to sell,' said Mr Petti.

'You're a rich man, you'll manage,' was my terse reply; for once I felt hard-hearted.

It didn't take long for the news to get round the manor, it never does in Soho, and people were shocked to discover that I had no shares in the place. Nick Lander, who had recently bought L'Escargot, was one of them. He invited me over for a drink and when he showed me round there was a party going on; quite a few of the guests had been my customers. I liked it but I was nervous, also tired and rather depressed; I wanted to give up. Louie had come with me and though not a lot was said on that evening I knew something was in the wind. A few days later Nick invited himself to my home, asking that Louie should be present. I knew they had had a confab in the kitchen during our visit to L'Escargot but Louie had said nothing of what was discussed.

'I've come to make you an offer,' said Nick, leaving an envelope for me to open after he had gone.

It was a very good offer but I was still undecided; after all, I had been working in the same place for thirty years and I felt I was too old for change. It was Alan Jay Lerner who persuaded me. He was having dinner with his wife-to-be, Liz Robertson, and he said, 'Go for it, Elena, it is just the change you need. You're far too young to settle down.'

It was a difficult time and certainly not eased by the tension between me and the management. I distributed the wages to the staff each week and while I was doing it for Christmas week 1979, Piero Luigi threw a cheque for £50 at me in front of them: my Christmas box; not even a pound a week for the year, not even popped into a card; there was no goodwill, it was horrible. Louie wanted to take it back but I said no, it will pay for our Christmas dinner; when you've worked as hard as I have all your life just to scrape a living you don't throw money away as a gesture of pride. But I said to myself, 'Elena, you're going.'

On New Year's Eve, Alan Koupe, a dear friend who had been horrified to learn that Aldo and I had had to walk home the previous year, came in to pick us up and take us home. Alan had been contemplating buying a restaurant in Covent Garden and had asked me if I would be interested in running it. As I said, I had been dithering for months over my future so I asked him that night whether he was going ahead with his venture and told him about my offer from Nick; I didn't want to double-cross either of them. Alan said no, he hadn't been able to raise the funds and was now interested in something else but he advised me to accept Nick's offer. He said he would put me in touch with a lawyer, as it was also about time I had somebody looking after me legally. He was right. I had no pension, no contract and no claims on the place I had worked for for thirty years. I was having to learn to deal with a different world – the world of the eighties – but through the kindness of Alan and James Pettigrew of the *Sunday Mirror* I was able to sort out all the wheeler-dealing.

By now Charlie Petti was getting a little past understanding what was going on, so I rang his wife Gracie asking her to explain my position and filled her in on the way I was being treated. Then I went to Charlie himself. He wanted to know what they could offer me to stay. Gently I told him it was too late, saying, 'Look Charlie you're a rich man, I've worked for wages all my life, and now I am being offered a share of the profits and much better hours. Ask yourself, Charlie, if we swapped seats, what your decision would be.'

And his answer was, 'You're right Elena.'

So I rang Nick and said, 'Yes, I'm coming,' and he dropped the phone with surprise.

I later heard that Mr Ricci scoffed round the manor, 'What does she think, that all her customers are going to follow her?' But that, my dears, is exactly what they did.

Seventeen

I could have taken a taxi into work on 2 June 1981, the day L'Escargot opened. I was sixty-one years old and for the first time in my life I was being paid a decent wage. But old habits die hard and as I sat on the number 38 bus I was excited and nervous as that kid of forty-seven years before started her first job with Mr Arnaldi in Mortimer Street.

Nick Lander had made sure we had plenty of publicity, and I had written to many customers telling them where to find me from now on, but I knew it was going to be a challenge. I myself clung to familiar habits like my old bus route and customers were creatures of habit too. To make them feel at home in new surroundings with quite a different style of food would take a lot of hard work. But with that curious instinct that is essential in the restaurant business, Nick was right, people were ready for a change. From the first day, when the place was filled with old friends like Michael Codron, Frank Czitanovich, Jack Andrews from Thames TV, Isobel Davie (Tommy Steele's manager) and Peter Watson who had helped rescue my friend Harry Calleia from a death sentence and now works for *Campaign*, L'Escargot was a success.

The nicest part of it was that the old friends cheerfully accepted the odd hiccup and it was just as well they were prepared to be indulgent as the first evening was an absolute nightmare. Now, I know it is a tradition in the States for 'resting' actors to do a little waiting at table to keep body and soul together, but nobody had told me that Clive Merrison and Caroline Hutchinson had been employed. They were both actors and old customers from Bianchi's and I loved them dearly, but not in their role as waiters on my first day, when I was still fighting with my own anxiety. How anybody got the meals they ordered that night I'll never remember. Clive has fortunately returned to the fold as an actor and now has enough work to keep him from under my feet forever; sadly, poor lovely Caroline died far too young, of cancer.

There was one waitress who earned a very unceremonious send-off from me. I cannot and will not waste energy on being vindictive, but when somebody tries to exploit my friends I really go to town. It all started when Ella Fitzgerald followed me from Bianchi's to L'Escargot. Of course, I was thrilled that she liked the new place and still wanted to sit around and have a chat, who wouldn't be? Now, I know that having worked hard as a waitress I have been fortunate enough to become a *maître d'*, very rare for a woman, but I also understand that many people, both male and female, use the job as a filler to provide for another career. So when this waitress told me it was her ambition to become a photographer I encouraged her. We have a great many famous names come in, and if they don't mind being snapped it's OK by me. One evening she had taken several pictures of Ella, Aldo and myself, when Ella spotted Gene Wilder sitting across the room and she asked the waitress if she had any more film in the camera. She turned to me and said, 'Would you ask him if he would have a picture taken with me?' Quite rightly,

Gene Wilder was immensely flattered and was across the room like lightning. The girl took a smashing picture, which I had framed.

A year later when Gene Wilder's wife, Gilda Radner, came in with Ruby Wax she begged for the picture to give her husband as a surprise Christmas present. But I demurred. I couldn't bear to part with it. The waitress said her boyfriend had a developer and she would get it copied for me. The girl returned the print but wouldn't part with the negative. I was furious and sacked her. I could guess what was coming next and sure enough I had a call from Mrs Wilder saying that she was receiving mysterious calls asking how much she would pay for the negative. I was horrified but there was nothing I could do as all the letters I sent her were returned unopened.

I told this tale of woe to an old friend, Stanley Bielecki, who worked for SB International and he said he would make enquiries. He knew all the picture-editors in Fleet Street and though it took him a long time he managed to track her down in the end, make an appointment and then told her to her face that what she was trying to do was illegal. The pictures were taken on somebody else's premises and nobody in Fleet Street would touch them (I don't know if this was bluff, but she must have believed him because she handed over the negative). Next time he came he was wreathed in smiles and carrying a large envelope with the negative in it. It was such a pleasure to be able to send Mrs Wilder her copy, at last. I had a sweet note of thanks from Gene Wilder, telling me that he had not been able to return to London as Gilda had been very ill with cancer but was responding to treatment very well; it made it all the more sad to read of her death a few months later.

Forty-odd years of working among people with precarious careers have in a roundabout way taught me to be an optimist. Fortunes do change in curious cycles and I've watched success disappear like water down a drain, and the blackest moments of failure turn from despair to happiness. I consider it part of my job – and, bless him, so did Aldo – to help people through the bad times. I never say 'told you so' when life changes for the better. I don't have to, my Soho people are too honest to need reminders.

Yes, it is easy to be optimistic for other people when you know their talents and have seen so many of them survive bad patches, but when it happened to me I thought my whole world had collapsed. I had been at L'Escargot for about two years. We were a tremendous success and a very happy team. I still kept long hours but I enjoyed them all and I had no financial worries. I was part of the blooming, booming eighties. Then one morning I missed my mouth taking a cup of tea, spilt it all down myself. Well, my dears, I've seen enough booze go down the front of shirts and dresses late at night as shaking hands have missed their owners' mouths, so I thought that perhaps I was just a bit overtired. Until I went into the bathroom and saw myself in the mirror... The whole of one side of my face had dropped: my left eye was sagging, my mouth was distorted. I called Aldo and his face was about as grey as mine when he saw me. I looked like a nightmare from some ghastly old horror film. I felt no pain – in fact I felt nothing, which is why I had not been able to swallow my tea.

With an instinct for which I will always be grateful I got on the bus and went to work, perhaps I thought it was some kind of nervous twitch that would have disappeared by the time I got there. I climbed up the stairs to the office and said to Nick Lander, 'Something strange has happened to my face.'

He took me straight round to a nerve specialist in Wimpole Street who diagnosed Bell's Palsy (an unfortunate name for a disease, particularly if the patient has never even liked the taste of whisky), the temporary paralysis of the facial nerves. Over the next few weeks it didn't feel at all temporary to me as I went through the daily electric shock treatment; the doctor informed me that the longer I could stand the pain the more rapid my recovery would be. He later told me I had been very brave – a compliment I accepted without mentioning that vanity and work were my spurs.

Meanwhile Jonathan Somper, Nick's assistant, had told me about his father who was a practitioner in homoeopathy and as I got better I started to consult him, something I still do regularly. Soon I was back in the best of health as well as at my place at the top of the stairs, with my energy completely restored.

Well, at least I'd practised what I'd preached – don't let the world get you down – and very happy I was to be back in harness when, a couple of years later, Westminster celebrated its four-hundredth anniversary; included in the celebrations was a garden party given by the Soho Restaurateurs' Association and a service at Westminster Abbey attended by the Queen.

Now, I first saw the Queen in 1953 when she went to some gala performance at Sadlers Wells in Rosebery

Avenue. The whole neighbourhood turned out, me with Louie in his pram – six months old, he was – and clutching Adriana, who was ten, by the hand. How we oohed and aahed and how we jostled, too, just to catch a glimpse, it was all so exciting. The next time I saw her was leaving the stage door of the Prince Edward Theatre; she had been there on a private visit and it was Freddy, the barrow 'boy' who had a fruit stall outside Bianchi's, who told us she was there. (Freddy was the eyes and ears of Soho and I still see his daughter Maureen at our church socials.) I can't quite remember how long the customers had to wait for their orders that night, but when Freddy alerted us we all poured into the street (Bianchi's is almost next door to the stage door, which is in Frith Street). There were Mary, Louisa and myself, gawping like teenagers, when along came a young copper who told us to move along. We had no intention of leaving our vantage point so we didn't budge; back he came, officious as very young coppers often are, possibly thinking that we were three ladies of the street. When we explained we were waitresses from Bianchi's who just wanted to see our Queen, he told us not to be cheeky. Can you imagine? We'd probably been working for our livings when he was still in short pants. Anyhow we stood our ground, which was right beside the stage-door exit, and at that moment the Queen, Prince Philip and a guest emerged, preceded by a very flustered manager who trod right on my foot, that's how close we were. My years of training prevented me from letting out an almighty yell of pain which might have startled Her Majesty, but the dressmaker in me can still remember every detail of her beautiful blue lace dress.

So when I received an invitation to take part in the

garden party for Westminster I was delighted to accept and be part of a royal occasion. The marquees were set up and everybody's best food was laid out looking decorative and stylish. Then the manager of L'Epicure, an old French restaurant in Romilly Street that still keeps the oil lamps flaming outside, discovered that I did not have a badge for the Westminster Abbey service. He was shocked that I who had worked in Soho longer than any of them and was also the only female *maître d'* on the manor should have been so overlooked. It didn't surprise me, I've worked with men for too long to expect them to think about anything but their own prestige or skins, but I was touched and flattered when he pinned his own badge to my dress. And so I found myself once again at a Church of England service among the aristocracy – and when I looked around, there, on the other side of the aisle, were Lady Wilson and her husband smiling at me.

After the service we went back to the garden party and suddenly Bill Heseltine, whom I had seen next to the Queen in the Abbey, was bearing down on me with the Queen's lady-in-waiting and she was asking all about Aldo and the children; then I heard Bill say, very politely to someone, 'May I borrow the Queen for a moment?' and before I could collect myself he was leading her towards me. My legs went to jelly and as she held her hand out to me all I could think was, 'For Christ's sake, curtsey, Elena!' and I think I more or less managed it.

'I'll never forgive you for catching me like that,' I scolded Bill afterwards. 'But I won't forget it, either.' The worst part of all was that there were no photographers around at that moment to snap us; I think I could have forgiven even that wicked, exploiting little waitress had she been on the spot at the time.

I guard my friendships jealously, but not in a personal sense. I love to introduce people (strictly on a business level, the other sort they can manage on their own, as I've noticed over the years), and I get upset when things are reported wrongly in the papers. I know gossip columnists have to make a living but when they threaten my reputation for discretion they get more than a flea in their ear; they get a very voluble phone call at their office and the one piece of information they were not looking for, which is not to try to book a table ever again. A young man from *Today* tried it recently. He came in without booking saying that he had been to a publication launch and could I find him a space. I had tables moved to make room for him – and he repaid me by listening in on my conversation with Michael and Mary Parkinson, two of my dearest old friends, and printing every word the following day. It is like inviting someone to your home and hearing later that they had noticed dust in the corners.

But when the ruffled and volatile Italian feathers have settled down I have to admit that the plus side of my life infinitely outpaces the minor disagreeablenesses. Sometimes late at night people say, 'When it comes down to it, you're lucky if you have four, at most five, true friends you could ring at any time of the day or night when you need help.' They prod their fingers, miss a few and reach for another slug of red wine or brandy. I have learned over the years not to remind them that up until fifteen minutes before they were surrounded by a very jolly company that they told to F off as they signed the bill. It's called boozer's gloom I believe. There should, in this world, be many friends deeply grateful for my discretion and understanding; I do not tell the moaner the telephone numbers of his best friends – there are times when everyone needs a good night's sleep. I just try to organise a taxi so their head will hit the pillow before it hits the pavement.

In 1986 I would have needed more than two sets of fingers and toes to count my friends; Michael Ivens decided to throw a party for me at L'Escargot in honour of the years he had known me. I was to be the guest in the Banqueting Room. It was gorgeous, all my dear friends from years back were there; the list would take a page but it did include Melvyn and Kate Bragg, George and Sally Baker, Moira Fraser and Roger Lubbock, Bernard Levin, Patrick Janson-Smith, Bob Ringwood, Andy Rork and his missus, Janice. Nick Garland had drawn a huge cartoon which everybody signed and it sits on my wall at the top of the stairs where I meet everyone. I am so proud of it, it is a reminder of such a special evening. And can I tell you something that made it extra special? Michael Ivens and his wife Kate organised it out of love and the people that wanted to be part of it were all happy to pay to give me a lovely evening – but in the end, Nick Lander seeing our enormous love and affection for each other, just stood there and said, 'The evening's on me.' And I'm not going to tell you if I had a little weep when I got home that evening, so there.

Dear Nick, the perfect boss to have as a partner even though he was of a different generation from me – or perhaps because because he was. He grew up in an age of equality I had certainly never known as a girl. When I was a young woman there would have been no question of a bank giving me a mortgage, let alone enough money to start my own business; it still continues to surprise people that I have never owned a place for myself. Indeed in the late fifties or early sixties if the bill was passed to a woman to pay I would become quite flustered. But I have adapted to equality the same way I've had to adapt to everything else. I mean, I know I learnt from Mama that women worked as hard as their husbands, but for a man to be seen accepting hospitality from a woman, well he was either a pimp or a gigolo. Ah well, we live and learn. And I did.

Nick was unstinting in his recognition of the help my connections gave him in making his restaurant a success, so it was absolute hell when I was called upstairs to the office one day because he had collapsed. He was ill, seriously ill – a young man with talent, warmth and style – and when one evening he called me to tell me he would have to sell, all I could say was, 'Your health must come first.'

So there I was, knocking on even more years (it should by rights have been the female equivalent of slippers and pipe for me for the last seven of them) when Nick invited me to meet one of the potential buyers of L'Escargot. It was a courteous gesture. Nick could have just sold it to the highest bidder at that time; he had turned Soho back into a fashionable area practically single-handed. When he bought that beautiful Queen Anne house in 1980 Soho was going through one of her sleazy periods, rife with porno-merchants selling very explicit magazines and displaying equally embarrassing pictures outside their cinemas. There were touts everywhere and a level of villainy that wasn't even interesting enough to be called Hogarthian. Nasty little people with loads and loads of money. Anyhow Nick Lander had had this dream of elegance which he had fulfilled and he wasn't going to let his illness interfere with it. So he introduced me to Mr Bassanini, the man who had once owned the Meridiana in the Fulham Road, one of those *trattorias* that had so worried Mr Bianchi in the late sixties.

Mr Bassanini simply said to me, 'If you will stay, I will buy.'

My sigh of relief was probably audible. I had no wish to give up working, still don't, but I had been nervous enough of the outcome of the meeting to bring Louie along as my adviser. Looking back, I'm not sure if I was being pompous or at last learning my own worth, but I said ever so grandly, 'I shall have to sleep on it.' All I know is that as Louie drove me home I felt a kind of odd satisfaction that the Italian–Soho connection was going to be maintained. Of course I was going to stay.

There was a lot of speculation in the papers about how much Mr Bassanini had paid, something over a million apparently, but then money has become an absurd game, hasn't it? When I think how Mama and Papa scrimped and saved to buy the house we live in for £900, and I look at the prices for similar houses on the market now and see they are worth somewhere near a quarter of a million, I am amazed.

It all seems so daft really because I still lead such a simple life, cooking Aldo's lunch before I leave for work – something he can put in the microwave I won from an *Evening Standard* competition. What would we do if we sold the house? Buy a geriatrics' retreat in Spain? Not our style. Our blood is bonded to Soho where at least no one is ever going to die of boredom.

After years of working day and night I now occasionally take an evening to enjoy a bit of the high life too, and I would be a hypocrite if I didn't admit that a bit of hobnobbing with the stars still gives me a childish thrill. It is fun when people like Kathy Evans go out of their way to arrange tickets and invite us backstage for drinks. She did for the last night of *Evita* and it was a very gala event with Tim Rice making a speech and handing out gifts to the cast. We met Kathy's family and, of course, her dear husband Peter Purvis, who is an old friend from his *Blue Peter* days. David Land made a speech too and afterwards came over to tell me that he considers L'Escargot his café now, which made the place sound as jolly and casual as my old Bianchi's.

David Land was also at the *Miss Saigon* première. What an evening that was! Cameron came in a couple of months beforehand and threatened that he would hold the whole thing up unless he knew I would be present on the first night. He was joking of course, but what a lovely way to issue an invitation. Aldo had bronchitis so Louie was my escort (Janice is very good at loaning him out when I need him) and as soon as we arrived we were taken by the theatre manager to the Green Room for drinks. Then after the show, which I thought was wonderful, we all got on a boat and went to the Cotton Club for an enormously lavish party. I didn't have to feel a bit overwhelmed by the glittering assembly as there were so many customers present and they all came over for a hug and a chat.

Another fine occasion was when Jessye Norman was recording her Christmas television show at Ely Cathedral. I went with Don Fraser, her arranger, and we all had instructions to wear our winter togs – although it was a hot July day; but even the agony of sweltering under arc lights couldn't detract from the gloriousness of that lovely lady's voice.

Albert Finney is another sweetheart who makes sure that we are properly looked after whenever he appears in the West End, always making sure the manager knows we are coming, that there are drinks for us in the interval and that we are personally conducted backstage afterwards. It is so thoughtful. When we went to see him in *Another Time* recently, there was a very happy session in his dressing-room with dear David de Keyser, who made my opening day at L'Escargot so special. We went out to dinner with Janet Suzman and Maurice Denham and fell to talking about the changes we have seen over the years, changes in manners and clothes particularly. Maurice told me that when he was a young actor no one would have been allowed to work backstage without a collar and tie.

I notice the difference too; there are young men who earn a small fortune in the advertising industry but you wouldn't know it from their turn-out – bomber jackets and battered trainer shoes. It doesn't worry me, though I suppose I didn't see a pair of jeans till the middle sixties. It is their uniform and if they feel at ease that's fine by me. It's not what people wear but who they are that counts, clothes don't make the person, manners do.

I haven't noticed a great deal of difference in the manners of my customers despite their change of dress, but I have seen an enormous change in drinking habits. The days of getting blotto at lunchtime disappeared in the ambitions eighties, probably due to a mixture of the threat of unemployment, an awareness of health, the passing of the years and the need to be alert for all the new technology. It is not at all unusual to see two men, dressed as casually as any poor soul on the dole, lunching together and drinking only mineral water. They aren't economising, just being careful of their health, wealth and status.

Manners on the street are a different matter altogether

and I'm not just talking about the filth thrown about from the take-away places. I don't think I have grown over-sensitive with age, but the way people barge along the pavements as if only they existed in the universe is offensive. Even more offensive is the way some kids behave today. Now, as I have said I'm quite small and getting on a bit, but I haven't forgotten my street *nous* from my Clerkenwell days, so when a couple of kids tried flashing at me as I was walking home alone one day I was able to turn on them and shout, 'If you think it's so pretty why don't you put a bloody bow on it.' It was they who got the shock not me, but it is indicative of the unpleasantness of not respecting other people's right to be alive.

So it's small wonder that I enjoy coming to work among people who, if they do fly off the handle sometimes, can be excused on the grounds of temperament not just blind rage against the world. Yes, I like the risk-takers, the ones who are prepared to put their talent on the line; they are usually people without bluster like Derek Jacobi, so shy and charming, or Ian McKellen, who once brought in a Russian friend, a poet I think, and pointed out the ring his friend was wearing; a magnificent diamond that had once belonged to Rasputin. They have all been part of my life, and I of theirs since our Bianchi days when we were all hard up. It would be presumptuous of me to compare myself to them and their achievements, but there is a mutual appreciation of effort that I find very rewarding. There are others too, like Danny La Rue who is also a child of Soho, an unassuming man who never forgets an old friend, and Peter Snow, who would always give me a lift into town if he spotted me at the bus stop.

Curiously it is that familiar old bus stop that keeps

my feet happily on the ground; it is there or along the route that I meet up with old friends from the neighbourhood who can check whether I am going to a certain social or dinner and dance to raise money for our charities (like a children's or old people's home). Of course I am; I couldn't become disconnected from my past or my religion.

My parents made sure that we children were never neurotic about religion. I know that aspects of Catholicism vary from country to country and that somehow the Irish were taught to be weighed down by guilt; I haven't made a study of it but I know the Italians, or at least the ones I was brought up with, have always accepted their religion with joy. I go to church every Sunday, not out of duty or fear, but for the pleasure and peace it gives me, and so do my friends. It is an oasis of a different kind of love which includes caring and feeling responsible for others in the community, truly something that was bred into us when we were young and less fortunate. It is hopefully a heritage from Mama and Papa that I have passed on to my own children and through them to my grandchildren. I know that religion is a very personal thing and something that has been in decline over the last few decades, but surprisingly even the most sceptical of people sometimes ask me to light a candle for a friend in trouble. It is then that I go to St Patrick's in Soho Square because I feel it is the right locality for the problem – sentimental possibly – but it feels right to me and when my prayers have been answered I am happy for the person who had the grace and love to ask.

Some people you don't have to pray for – not that they haven't been unhappy. Jeffrey Bernard is a perfect example. I was reminded a few weeks back when an actor friend came in after the first night of the play Keith Waterhouse wrote about Jeff called *Jeffrey Bernard is Unwell*. Nicholas Bennet, the actor, told me how great it was and how excellent Peter O'Toole was as Jeff, and my mind sped back years to a time when I found Jeff sobbing on the stairs after a telephone call. I don't know which woman it was in his life who had made him so desperately unhappy but I always had an instinct about him; he would be all right because he was a survivor. I was also immensely pleased to hear the first reports of the play's success; it involved three dear customers for a start and my dearly beloved Soho was its setting.

Although I now read the reviews of all the plays and films, there are times when I can predict what the papers are going to say from the reactions of customers. If they have rung and booked a table for a first night and turn up early I know it is going to go down the drain; it always makes me feel a bit sad because I know the amount of effort that goes into every production. I've listened to so many hopes.

Not all my friends are household names. Many of my oldest customers have moved out of London now and I only see them once a year or so, but they too have followed me to L'Escargot and their visits are times for laughter and reminiscing. People like Shirley and Jack Trefusis, whose son Charles organises an annual opera reunion party at L'Escargot. Jack first came to Bianchi's in 1952 with a friend, Geoffrey Pinnock, a man whose only son had been killed in Italy during the war, a terrible loss. Mr Pinnock used to make a pilgrimage to the place where his boy was killed every year, and there he was befriended by an Italian family who were related to Mr Bianchi. It was a solace to him and for us it was the beginning of a friendship that has lasted over three decades.

There are others too, like Sheila Plowman who used to bring her art-student son Chris and his friend Tim Mara in for lunch – and they were always happy, laughing affairs. She also lives in the country now but when she was up last she reminded me about the time she brought a friend who, poor soul, had lost half a leg in a road accident. When he was fitted up with an artificial limb, Sheila decided to take him out for a celebration lunch at Bianchi's to practise going up the stairs. He managed very well, sat down and they ordered their meal. They had just finished their starters, when her friend suddenly said, 'It's no use, Sheila, I'll have to take it off for a while; it's too damn painful.' Sheila assured him it was OK by her so he unstrapped it and stood it up beside the table. It was a touch too realistic, with shoe and sock and a bit of knee, and it very nearly gave the waiter apoplexy when he arrived at the table to serve the main course.

Seeing Sheila again also reminded me of just how many artists used to use Bianchi's. James Fitton and his wife spent their fiftieth wedding anniversary there with James Boswell and his wife. James Boswell painted a picture of the fruit stand called *Il Ricordo di Bianchi* which was shown at the Royal Academy Summer Exhibition. Craigie Aitchison used to come in with his dog; he had bought it a jewelled collar but led it on either a piece of string or an old tie. Wouldn't be allowed now under the new health rules; the only dog we are able to accept in the restaurant belongs to David Blunkett, the blind MP. Another dear artist friend is Jennie Poggi who sends me a hand-painted card each Christmas which I frame. I had watched her fall in, out of and in love again with the same man, and one day they came in to announce that two weeks before they had had a baby boy and that they had just come from getting married; what was more, they told me that the boy's middle name was to be Aldo (if the child had been a girl it would have been Elena). I was so happy for them. I was not so happy when, a couple of years later, they split up – but very proud to possess pictures of Ziggi Aldo in my albums, another generation of my extended family.

When I was young distance meant days of travelling or weeks for letters to arrive; now, I am as likely to see people who commute between America and Europe more often than those who live in the country. International jobs seem to mean catching almost as many planes as I do buses. It also appears that the kind of people who have Soho connections are going to end up in similar places all over the world. Nigel Cooper, an advertising executive who was a Bianchi fan and now lives in Beverley Hills, always calls when he is in London and told me how he found himself all alone in Milan one New Year's Eve. He looked up the most fashionable restaurant and asked the *maître d'* if there was room for one; the *maître d'* replied in a sort of broken London-Italian accent that sounded familiar to Nigel so he asked where he came from; of course, it was Soho and the man had worked at Bianchi's. Apparently they fell on each other; Nigel passed on all the news about me and was given the best table and feasted on a fourteen-course meal. Lovely to think of being a bond to two strangers on a New Year's Eve.

I read in the quotes from Jeffrey Bernard's play that he sometimes feels that he is sitting beside the deathbed of Soho. I can't agree. She ain't dying yet, not if you look at the heart of Soho which is its people – its devotees, if you like. Yes, there are changes at street level – silly T-shirt shops where there used to be family shops – but most of the streets have not been altered and turned into precincts like the centres of many country towns. The only two tower blocks house real locals, people whose early childhood was as hard as mine, and I bet they don't mind having indoor plumbing in their old age any more than I do. The markets flourish – and if the traders who work such long hours take more exotic holidays than their parents could have dreamed of, why not?

Of course, I am sad at some of the changes and I miss many of the old characters – Mr Bossi for a start, and people like Frankie Blake who became the first wrestling compère on television and told the most terrible jokes. He used the Café Bleu and used to call me the Duchess of Soho; in a way he kind of personified Soho in that he arrived at the age of fourteen from Liverpool and never looked beyond the area. He knew every minor villain in the business and lived in a flat above Pattisserie Valerie from which he would descend each morning in his dressing-gown for his croissants and coffee. The fact that his brother was Father Peter of Farm Street in Mayfair didn't disturb his conscience a great deal, but it certainly made him one of us.

I miss some of the craziness lent to the early years by people like John Nicholls, who once came in to apologise for some previous bad behaviour and was again so drunk he gave me a cauliflower instead of flowers, and D'Arcy Conyers who could turn any meal into a riot. I'm sorry, too, that Gaston Berlemont has retired from the French Pub, even though I only went in there once in my life. Like me, he travelled in every day by public transport and when he closed his upstairs restaurant I used to send his favourite dish of *osso bucco* round to him from Bianchi's.

Soho has been the focal point of my life, after my family, and it still hasn't lost it's magic for me – nor for a lot of people judging by the influx of the younger generation. They in turn are making careers and reputations for themselves; some will succeed and others will suffer heartbreak just as it has always been as far as I have seen. Soho has always been home to the drifters as well as the hard grafters, the lucky and the unlucky; it has its devious side as well as its charm and in that way it will never really change.

Here I have been given a good life with more warmth, friendship and laughter than any little girl from the back streets of Clerkenwell could have dreamed of; I hope I have given enough back to keep my beloved Soho alive. Just as the Italians play *briscola* every Sunday morning in Soho's Coach & Horses as happily and noisily as ever, so the streets of Soho still echo with snatches of Italian which tell me I'm home from home.

Index

Abbott, Bud, 68
Abey, Dennis, 114–15, 116–17
Adelina, Madame, 144–6
Adler, Larry, 15, 41
Aitchison, Craigie, 178
Aitken, Maria, 130
Alex (waiter), 146
Algeria, 136–7
Algerian Wine Stores, 56
Ali, Tariq, 117
Ameche, Don, 41
Amies, Hardy, 87–8
Amis, Kingsley, 153
Amis, Martin, 153
Andke, Stefan, 130–1
Andrew, Prince, 5–6
Andrews, Anthony, 150
Andrews, Georgina, 150
Andrews, Jack, 11, 162
Annabel's, 31
Arandora Star, 45, 46
Archer, David, 100
Arden, Paul, 151
Arnaldi, Mr, 37–9, 162
Ayer, Freddie, 76

Bach, Barbara, 16–17
Bacon, Francis, 4, 100
Bacuzzi, Joe, 27
Baird, John Logie, 153
Baird, Mrs John Logie, 153
Baker, George, 8, 111, 170
Baker, Hilda, 94

Baker, Sally, 8, 170
Balon, Norman, 59
Banham, Derek, 115
Bar Italia, 2
Basillio, Carmen, 118
Bassanini, Mr, 171–2
Baxter, Stanley, 88
BBC, 108
Beecham, Sir Thomas, 39
Behan, Brendan, 100
Behrens, Tim, 96
Bell, David, 157
Beloff, Nora, 73
Benini, 45
Bennet, Nicholas, 176
Bennett, Alan, 103, 109–10
Berg, Jack Kid, 118
Berlemont, Gaston, 56, 180
Berlemont, Victor, 56
Berlin, Sir Isaiah, 76
Bernard, Bruce, 59, 100
Bernard, Jeffrey, 59, 100, 176–7, 179
Betjeman, John, 121–2
Bianchi, Mr, 46, 67, 69, 74, 119, 133, 143, 156, 177
Bianchi's, 2, 3, 4, 67–102, 112–40, 146–61, 178
Bielecki, Stanley, 164
Bifulco, 156
Binchy, Maeve, 7
Binelli brothers, 9
Blake, Frankie, 180

Bligh, Sir Timothy, 73, 90, 129
Blunkett, David, 178
Blunt, Sir Anthony, 76
Bossi, Mr, 46, 55, 58–9, 64, 180
Boswell, James, 178
Bourke-Sheridan, Marguerite, 69–70
Bourne and Hollingsworth, 38, 48
Boyars, Marion, 99
Boyd, Patti, 16–17
Bragg, Kate, 170
Bragg, Melvyn, 19, 123, 170
Brahms, Caryl, 102
Brett, Jeremy, 130, 141
Brian (son-in-law), 125
Britten, Tony, 71, 125
Broderick, John, 98–9
Brown, Gaye, 10–12
Brown, Georgia, 146
Browne, Coral, 4
Bruce, Mr, 98
Buckingham Palace Press Office, 75–6
Bull, Peter, 84–5
Burgess, Guy, 76
Butler, Rab, 73
Buzzards, 49

Café Bleu, 2, 55–61, 64, 67, 88, 142, 180
Café Luxembourg, New York, 103
Callan, Paul, 133
Callas, Maria, 68–9
Calleia, Harry, 136–7, 162
Cambridge Theatre, 61
Camillo, Father, 101
Campari Club, 88
Campbell, Michael, 111
Cardus, Sir Neville, 82–3
Carradine, David, 18–19
Casson, Lewis, 68
Cavalli's, 88
Cavallo, Pete, 122–3, 124

Centrepoint, 101
Chamberlain, Neville, 42
Chaplin, Patricia, 96–7
Chardet, Tony, 125–6
Charlie's, New York, 102–3
Chez Auguste, 141–2
Churchill, Sir Winston, 43, 45, 46, 61, 70
Clapton, Eric, 16
Clive, 87–8
Coach and Horses, Back Hill, 27, 28
Coach & Horses, Greek Street, 59, 181
Codron, Michael, 162
Coldstream, Sir William, 76
Collins Music Hall, 41
Colquhoun, Robert, 100
Colville, Sir Richard, 75–6
Connery, Sean, 71
Connie, 'Aunt', 62
Conyers, D'Arcy, 130, 180
Conyers, Jilly, 130
Cook, Peter, 21–2, 153
Cooper, Henry, 118
Cooper, Nigel, 179
Cooper, Tommy, 88
Cornish, Mr, 92
Cornthwaite, Graham, 147
Cornwell, David, 72
Costello, Lou, 68
Cotton Club, 173
Cranium Club, 76
Crisp, Quentin, 112
Cusack, Sinead, 150
Czitanovich, Frank, 12, 155, 162

Daily Mirror, 33, 88, 109
Daily Telegraph Magazine, 132
Dalli, Toni, 71
Daly, Isobel, 82
Dame Alice Owen's School, 53
Dankworth, Johnny, 4, 102

Davie, Isobel, 162
Davies, Sergeant, 70
De Gaulle, Charles, 74
De Havilland, Olivia, 41
De Keyser, David, 5, 173–4
De Marney, Derek, 58
De Marney, Terence, 58
Debenham and Freebody's, 48
Delano, Tony, 12
Delmonico, 156
Dempster, Nigel, 12, 133
Dench, Judi, 14–15
Denham, Maurice, 174
Di Maggio, Joe, 39
Di Maggio, Nimfa, 39, 45, 48
Diana, Princess of Wales, 49, 136
Dickens, Charles, 28
Dimes, Albert, 63, 74–5, 88, 93
Dino (nephew), 105, 108
Diplock, Dippy, 152
Dorville, Admiral, 59
Dorville Models, 37–8
Douglas, Melvyn, 41
Driver, Winnie, 63–4
Dugdale, Brian, 8–9
Dundee, Angelo, 118
Dundee, Chris, 118
Dunera, 46
Dunkirk, 43
Dunaway, Faye, 97–8

E & G Stores, 2
Edward, Prince, 6
Edwards, Jimmy, 88
Elizabeth II, Queen, 74, 75–6, 166–8
Elliot, Denholm, 130
Elliot, Susie, 130
Elvin, Jack, 90, 91, 121
Emmanuel, David, 49
Emmanuel, Elizabeth, 49
L'Epicure, 167–8
Epstein, Brian, 107

Equity, 61
L'Escargot, 2–22, 159–61, 162–74
Establishment Club, 100, 102
Evans, Kathy, 172
Evening Standard, 172

Fame, Georgie, 147
Farson, Daniel, 100
Fascio Party, 44
Faye, Alice, 41
Feast of Our Lady of Mount Carmel, 31
Felixstowe, 32
Fenn, Michael, 13
Ferguson, Father, 101
Fever Hospital, Hampstead, 6
Finch, Peter, 97
Finney, Albert, 85, 153, 173–4
First World War, 45
Firth, Mrs, 146
Fisher, Danny, 12
Fitton, James, 178
Fitzgerald, Ella, 122–5, 163–4
Flanagan, Tony, 123
Foreign Office, 46
Forenson, Papa, 138–9
Fortnum and Mason, 22
Fortuna, Mr, 1, 2
France, 43, 58
Fraser, Don, 11, 173
Fraser, Moira, 170
Freddy (barrow boy), 94, 167
French Pub (York Minster), 56, 180

Gable, Clark, 41
Gall, Sandy, 153
Galway, Kay, 3
Garbon, Garry, 136–7
Gardner, Judge Edward, 8
Garland, Nick, 170
Gaston's, 90
Gazzano, Mr, 46

Geldof, Bob, 12
Gennarro's, 1–2
George VI, King, 27
Germany, 42, 43
Giardello, Joey, 118
Gielgud, Sir John, 21, 132
Gigli, Benjamino, 27–8, 70
Gillman, Peter and Leni, 46
Giorgio (waiter), 143, 144–5
Goldsmith, James, 77
Good, Des, 9–10
Gowing, Sir Lawrence, 76
Great Ormond Street Hospital, 6–7
Griffiths, Brian, 9–10
Groves, Sir Charles, 116
Grundy, Bill, 82–3
Guinness, Henrietta, 80–1

Hadley, Tony, 31
Hall, Ron, 134
Halliwell, Kenneth, 104–10
Hamilton, Gerald, 78
Hancock, Tony, 3
Hargreaves, Alan, 139
Harlech, Lord, 130
Harvey, Laurence, 87
Hastings, 42
Haw-Haw, Lord, 59
Hawkins, Miss, 76
Hawkyard, Tom, 5
Heath, Edward, 129
Helvetia, 56, 57
Heseltine, Bill, 75–6, 90, 136, 168
Heyward, Biddy, 6
Heyworth, Tania, 94–5
Hill, David, 91
Hiss, Alger, 155
Hitler, Adolf, 50, 59
Hobbs, Jack, 40
Holborn Empire, 41
Home Office, 46
House of Commons, 8

Humphries, Barry, 128–9
Hurt, John, 4, 73, 111–12, 129–30
Hutchinson, Caroline, 163
Hyman, Mrs, 74–5

Idle, Eric, 14
Ingrams, Richard, 133, 153
Irons, Jeremy, 150
Isaacs, Jeremy, 123, 157
Isherwood, Christopher, 78
Isherwood, Liz, 11
Islington Empire, 41
Italy, 43, 63
ITV, 108
Ivens, Kate, 89–90, 170
Ivens, Michael, 18, 89–90, 170
Izzard, Bryan, 84, 93–4

Jackson, Anne, 154–5
Jacobi, Derek, 175
Janson-Smith, Patrick, 170
Jolliffe, Gray, 146–7
Jourdan, Louis, 86
Joyce, Quentin, 59–60, 114
Joyce, William, 59
Julie, 35–6
Juliet (sister), 24–5

Kee, Robert, 13
Kelly, Miss, 31
Kendall, Kay, 97
Kennedy, Caroline, 17–18
King, Pete, 93
Kirkpatrick, Father Bill, 101
Kleinman, Philip, 152–3
Koupe, Alan, 160

La Rue, Danny, 175
Labour Party, 121
Laine, Cleo, 4, 102
Land, David, 173
Lander, Nick, 159, 160–1, 162, 166, 170–1

186

Langton, Diane, 11
Laughton, Charles, 86
Lawson, George, 81
Le Carré, John, 72
Le Mesurier, John, 80
Leighton, Margaret, 67–8, 71
Lerner, Alan Jay, 159
Leventon, Anabel, 11
Levin, Bernard, 170
Lewis, John, 38, 48, 64–5
Lieberson, David, 14
Lieberson, Sandy, 5, 14
Livings, Henry, 153
Logan, Andrew, 12
London School of Economics, 117
Louisa (cousin), 40
Lowry, Emma, 150
Lowry, Judge Nina, 8, 149–50
Lowry, Judge Richard, 149–50
Lowry, Stephen, 150
Loy, Myrna, 41
Lubbock, Roger, 170
Luckwell, Mike, 115, 156
Lugano, 63
Lumley, Joanna, 11
Lynn, Vera, 41

MacBryde, Robert, 100
McCallum, David, 87
McCarthy, Joe, 155
McDermott, Miss, 30
McDowell, Malcolm, 147
McGuinn, Linda, 18
McKay, Peter, 133
McKellen, Ian, 153, 175
MacKintosh, Cameron, 125–6, 173
McKuen, Rod, 8
Maclean, Donald, 76–7
Maclean, Melinda, 76–7
Macmillan, Harold, 73
McNally, Keith, 103
McQueen, Steve, 139
Mafia, 138

Maggi, 45
Mama, 24–6, 30, 32, 33, 35, 36, 37, 48, 50–1, 55, 59, 60, 62, 64–5
Mann, Peggy, 47, 49–50
Mara, Tim, 177
Marciano, Rocky, 118
Marco (waiter), 127
Margaret, Sister, 30
Mario (brother), 47–8, 108
Mary (friend), 63
Mary (waitress), 86
Matthews, Kerwin, 85–6
Mavroleon, Nicky, 17
Melly, George, 100, 107
Meridiana, 171
Merrison, Clive, 163
MI5, 44
MI6, 140
Milan, 63, 179
Miller, Max, 41
Mitchell, Sir Derek, 72–3, 129
Molina, Alfred, 110
Moore, Dudley, 21–2
Morgan, John, 130
Movietone News, 42
Moving Picture Company, 115, 156
Mussolini, Benito, 43, 44; daughter, 33

Nerman, Einer, 131–2
Nero, Franco, 127
New York, 102–3
Newman, Nanette, 19–20
Nicholls, John, 180
Nixon, Richard, 155
Nolan, Mrs Sydney, 128
Norman, Frank, 86–7
Norman, Jessye, 173
Novello, Ivor, 131

Observer, 140
Odeon, Broadway, 103

187

O'Donnell, John, 147
O'Hara, Maureen, 41
Oldman, Gary, 110
Oltman, Willem, 135–6
Onassis, Christina, 17
Onassis, Jackie, 18
O'Neill, Terry, 97–8
Orr, James, 73–4, 75–6, 83, 129
Orton, Joe, 104–10
Osborne, Charles, 131
Oswald, Lee Harvey, 135
O'Toole, Peter, 176
Owen, David, 12
Owen, Deborah, 12

Paccini, Mr, 58, 64, 67, 70
Paccini, Mrs, 67
Page, Elaine, 3
Palin, Michael, 14
Palmer, Lili, 69
Papa, 24, 25–6, 35, 36, 42, 44–5, 48, 50–1, 59, 62, 64
Parker, Dr, 16
Parker, Lady, 95–6
Parker, Lord Chief Justice, 95–6
Parkinson, Mary, 169
Parkinson, Michael, 169
Parkinson, Norman, 5
Parmagina, 156
Pastrano, Willie, 118
Patino, Isobel, 77
Pattisserie Valerie, 180
Pep, Willie, 118
Peter, Father, 180
Petti, Charlie, 31, 92–3, 124, 141, 152, 156, 158, 160
Petti, Gracie, 160
Pettigrew, James, 160
Philip, Prince, 74, 167
Phillips, Brian, 28
Pierina (waitress), 86
Piero (manager of Bianchi's), 92–3, 144

Pike, Major, 147–8
Pike, Mrs, 146, 147–8
Pini, Serefino, 46
Pinnock, Geoffrey, 177
Pitt, Terry, 121–2
Plowman, Chris, 177
Plowman, Sheila, 177–8
Poggi, Jennie, 178–9
Police, 19
Polledri, Mr, 46
Polledri, Nino, 46
Pound, Pelham, 73
Power, Tyrone, 41
Price, Vincent, 3–4
Prince, Hal, 15
Pritchard, Barry, 109
Purvis, Peter, 172–3
Puttnam, David, 14

Quaglino's, 107

Radner, Gilda, 164
Raki, Mr, 99
Rampagna, Dr, 1, 32, 44
Rasputin, 175
Rattigan, Terence, 106
Raynor, Mr, 95
Redgrave, Michael, 58
Redgrave, Vanessa, 127
Reggiori's, 50
Reid, Beryl, 3, 83
Remick, Lee, 9–10
Resteghini's, 28
Reynolds, Stanley, 12
Ricci, Mrs, 161
Ricci, Nino, 137, 156–8
Ricci, Piero Luigi, 157–9
Rice, Tim, 172
Rice-Davies, Mandy, 73
Riddle, Nelson, 125
Rigg, Diana, 130
Ringwood, Bob, 125, 170
Riviera, Marieka, 87

Rix, Brian, 130
Robertson, Liz, 159
Rock Bottom, 10–11
Rogers, Ginger, 41
Romeo (brother), 50
Romero, Cesare, 41
Ronnie Scott's Club, 93, 97–8, 122–3, 124, 142
Rork, Andy, 116–17, 170
Rork, Janice, 116, 170
Ross, Annie, 146
Rothschild, Sir Charles, 152
Roy, Harry, 41
Royal Academy Summer Exhibition, 178
Royal Opera House, 53, 98

St Margaret's Church, Westminster, 129
St Patrick's, 176
St Peter's Italian Church, 27–8, 50, 101, 112
St Peter's Italian School, 26–7, 30–1, 35
Saltzman, Arnold, 13–14
Salvoni, Adriana (Elena's daughter), 6, 49, 53–4, 55, 64, 109, 125
Salvoni, Aldo (Elena's husband), 3, 15, 22–3, 24, 25, 32, 33, 38, 40–1, 42, 47–8, 50–2, 55, 64, 87, 94, 104, 107–8, 137–8
Salvoni, Anselma, 32, 102, 125
Salvoni, Jannette, 124, 173
Salvoni, Louie (Elena's son), 6, 70, 104–6, 108, 111–12, 124, 126, 159, 172, 173
Salvoni, Matthew, 64–5, 124–5
Sampson, Antony, 73
San Carlos Opera House, 61
Saville, Philip, 86
Sayle, Murray, 133, 134–5
Schofield, Paul, 84

Scott, Selena, 119
Second World War, 42–53, 58–61
Servardo, Gaia, 12
Shaw, Dennis, 79–80
Shell, 8–9
Shelton, Anne, 41
Sherrin, Ned, 12, 102–3
Shilling, David, 11
Shrub, Derek, 18
Sidoli, Lena, 40
Sidoli, Mr, 63
Signoret, Simone, 87
Sirs, Bill, 121
Sleep, Wayne, 11, 81
Snow, Peter, 175
Snows (flower shop), 49
Soho Brasserie, 56
Soho Restaurateurs' Association, 166
Soho Society, 156
Somper, Jonathan, 166
Sorrento's, 88
Sovrani, 45
Spandau Ballet, 31
Spanish Betty, 144–6
Spectator, 83
Spencer-Lewis, Dr, 47
Spender, Stephen, 76
Spot, Jack, 63, 74–5
Stander, Lionel, 86
Starr, Ringo, 16–17
Steele, Barbara, 11–12
Steele, Tommy, 162
Stewart, Alayne, 5
Stewart, Mr, 20–1
Sting, 19
Straker, Peter, 12
Street-Porter, Janet, 12
'Strega', Mr, 119–21
Summers, Anthony, 133–4
Sunday Dispatch, 78
Sunday Mirror, 160
Sunday Times, 136, 152–3

189

Suzman, Janet, 174
Switzerland, 63

T, Georgie, 31
Tambimuttu, 78–9
Tatler, 131–2
Taylor, Bill, 91
Taylor, John, 89–91, 121
Taylor, Robert, 41
Taylor, Shaw, 10
Ted's Cafe, 39, 42
Terry, Christopher, 154
Terry, Graham, 154
Thames TV, 10–11
Thomas, Dylan, 100
Thompson, Ken, 128, 131, 147
Thorndike, Dame Sybil, 68
Thorpe, Will, 118
Today, 169
Tollemarche, Miss, 39
Tomalin, Claire, 134–5
Tomalin, Nick, 4, 133, 134–5
Trefusis, Charles, 177
Trefusis, Jack, 177
Trefusis, Shirley, 177
Turpin, Dick, 28

Valentino, Rudolf, 40
Victor, Ed, 12–13
Villa Cesare, 93

Walach, Eli, 154–5
War Office, 46

Ward, Stephen, 73
Waterhouse, Keith, 176
Watson, Peter, 136, 162
Wax, Ruby, 164
Westminster Abbey, 166, 168
Westminster Council, 156
White, Michael, 12
Wilder, Gene, 163–4
Wilding, Michael, 67–8
Williams, Finty, 15
Williams, Michael, 14–15
Wilson, Gerry, 138–9
Wilson, Giles, 122
Wilson, Harold, 72
Wilson, Lady, 121–2, 168
Wilson, Sandy, 131
Wilton, Rob, 41
Wishing Well Appeal, 6–7
Wolfers, John, 94

Yates, Paula, 12
York, Duchess of, 6
York, Susannah, 153–4
York Minster (French Pub), 56, 180
Yudkin, Cis, 155

Zangiacomi, 45
Zavattoni, 45
Zetterling, Mai, 147
Zomparelli, Tony, 141
Zuckerman, Solly, 76